LETTERS

— VOLUME 1 —

ROSE OF SHARON

Ark House Press
arkhousepress.com

© 2023 Sharon Joy Webster

Unless otherwise stated, all Scriptures are taken from the New Living Translation (Holy Bible. New Living Translation copyright© 1996, 2004, 2007, 2013 by Tyndale House Foundation. Used by permission of Tyndale House Publishers Inc., Carol Stream, Illinois 60188. All rights reserved.)

Cataloguing in Publication Data:
Title: Alpha & Omega Letters Volume 1
ISBN: 978-0-6450375-2-4 (pbk)
Subjects: Christian Living; Spirituality;
Other Contributors: Webster, Sharon Joy

Design by initiateagency.com

TABLE OF CONTENTS

1. I Am With You Always 1
2. You Are A First Fruit 3
3. Seek Me In The Garden Of Eden 5
4. Without Love You Become As Nothing 12
5. I Am The Resurrected Christ 14
6. Little By Little You Become Christ-Like 17
7. *Alpha & Omega Board Game*® Revealed 21
8. Proclaim The Lord's Will In Your life 27
9. Anointed One Who Died For You 30
10. Enter And Sit At The Father's Feet 34
11. Show You New Revelations 38
12. Be Open To Hearing My Spirit 40
13. I Was Willing To Die In Your Stead 42
14. Heart For God 46
15. I Am Here In Spirit 49
16. Hope And Glory 52
17. Remember Your Creator 54
18. My Master Plan For Mankind 57
19. Perfect In His Eyes 59

20. I Am Here, Right By Your Side. 64
21. My Love Shall Cover The Land. 66
22. I Have Never Left You, Nor Forsaken You 69
23. Only Believe. 72
24. Prayer To Approach God In Heaven. 74
25. New Creation In Christ 78
26. No Longer Yearn With An Empty Heart 81
27. Direct Access To God The Father 83
28. Prepare For My Second Coming. 88
29. My Love Will Pour Forth 91
30. Wine Into New Wineskins. 94
31. God Created The Family Unit 98
32. My Birth Marks The Beginning 101
33. The Time Is NOW To Seek The Lord. 104
34. The Garden Of Eden Is About To Be Opened 107
35. My Love Will Go Out And Conquer The Evil One 112
36. Satan Knows He Has But Little Time. 116
37. Out Of Egypt And Into The Promised Land. 120
38. My Love Shall Fill The Void 127
39. It Is Through Belief That All May Enter 134
40. Create A New Heart. 139
41. The Veil Is Removed. 143
42. Approach The Throne Of Grace With Confidence 150
43. Enter Into God's Glorious Throne Room 155

*"I am the Alpha and the Omega
the First and the Last
the Beginning and the End" (Rev. 22:13)*

DEDICATION

I would like to thank God, Jesus and Holy Spirit for the precious gift of love and physical and Eternal life. "God is love" (1 John 4:16)

I would like to dedicate Volume 1 to my inspirational Mother, who allowed me to experience the amazing love of God through her unconditional love and to my faithful Father, who taught me reverence and obedience towards the omnipotent God and his precious Word and laws.

I would also like to sincerely thank my amazing children, Ross, Isaac, Brice and Clairissa for their love and patience; my five brothers and their partners, especially Gary and his wife Nancy; my coffee and prayer partner Kym and my closest forever friends who have helped encourage me on this 23 year venture.

I also deeply thank and acknowledge my three Editors who have also helped me complete this journey; my thoughtful and gifted brother, inspirational Sarah Cheesman, and multi-talented Chris Wyman.

Deepest heartfelt thanks to Nicole and her team at Ark House Press for their patience and help. Lastly special thanks to innovative Russ Scott for the *Alpha & Omega Board Game*® prototype.

44.	Put That Belief Into Action By Doing.	159
45.	Enter Through To The Holy Of Holies.	164
46.	There Is A New Day Dawning	168
47.	I Hurt To See You Hurting.	174
48.	Seek Me First	177
49.	Spirit Of Power.	181
50.	Total Heartfelt Commitment	184

Salvation Prayer 187

LETTER 1

I Am With You Always

My dearest child,

I want you to endure and be strengthened through these troubled times, knowing that I am with you always, even 'til the end.

I have allowed you to experience these deeply emotional and sometimes turbulent times in order to draw you closer to me.

I love you and I am fashioning you into a prized vessel that will bring many sons and daughters to glory. Have faith little child, believe it is me. I know in your heart you believe; now you must act, becoming a doer, not just a hearer. Time is drawing near when I require a total commitment from you. You will go through much testing but will come through strengthened and empowered by the Holy Spirit.

Please believe me when I say, "Fear not," and be ye anxious for nothing, little child, for your Father loves you and cares for you as he does for all the flowers in the field. Stand fast and stay close to God and he will guide you. He sent me so that you could have life and life much more abundantly.

The Spirit is given without measure as a helper to allow you to endure the hardships ahead.

Humble yourself and allow God to glorify you at my return, where you will enter into the Kingdom he has prepared for you. Know that it is I, Jesus Christ, who has spoken to you tonight. I died so that you may have life Eternal.

Be strong, my child with the strength that I will give to you. You are my child in whom I am well pleased. Continue to lay your treasure in Heaven where no moth or rust can destroy (Matt. 6:20) and know that I am here by your side and will carry you through the troubled times ahead.

You have been chosen to partake in the calling of many sons and daughters who I am leading and guiding. Your part is to feed them with knowledge and understanding of how they may come to God the Father through me, the crucified one. Celebrate and cry out for joy, little child, for the time of rejoicing is near.

Lean your heart towards God and yield your ways to him and he will give you the desires of your heart.

Now as for the *Alpha & Omega Board Game®*, indeed it is an instrument to be used by God to lead and teach those who hunger and thirst after God and his way of life; those who desire to come to his Throne of grace. The rules for this game that you now know about will be given when you have open ears, hungry to hear.

Shabbat Shalom

LETTER 2

You Are A First Fruit

My dearest child,

Listen to what God has to tell you. I want you to live your life in such a way that is pleasing to God. Listen and heed what he has to say in the Word and do what he requires of you. He is the great Shepherd and he gathers his sheep together to feed them and protect them from the hungry wolves that prowl around; seeking to devour any unsuspecting Lamb that may wander from the flock. Stay close to the flock. Don't wander away lest the temptation to go astray falls upon you.

Take heed, the Shepherd will protect you from any calamity but you must do your part. Beware, Satan is out to kill and destroy (John 10:10) and would love to have your soul today. DO NOT LET HIM. Flee from him, and he will leave you. This is a most serious and urgent matter—do not listen to his prejudices and deceiving lies.

God wholeheartedly desires to give you his precious Holy Spirit without measure to enable you to do his work, bringing many sons and daughters to glory. Be on fire for him, and the Gospel of his coming Kingdom. You are a first fruit and as such, are being tested to produce a commodity more precious than gold or silver, an imperishable reward to be given at my return.

Stay close to God. Don't let Satan get a foothold lest he devours you completely. Do not be mocked, he is serious about destroying your soul and will continue day and night; so stay close to the Shepherd and his chosen flock. It is much harder for Satan to attack you when you are closely guarded and under God's protective wing (Ps. 91:4)

My child, you are most precious to me. Don't give up. Stay close to God. He will never leave you nor forsake you. Grace, mercy and peace I leave with you. Be strengthened by his Spirit and be of good cheer. The day quickly approaches when you will be transformed by my Spirit and you will see God's glory face-to-face. Meanwhile God has placed you on this earth, predestined for a purpose. This will become more evident as time goes on.

Don't give up but be filled with the Spirit and be ye transformed by the renewing of your mind through my Word.

Peace I leave with you my trustworthy and faithful servant. Oh ye of little faith—why do you question every time I speak with you? Believe and be bold. Continue in good works bringing praise to God.

Shabbat Shalom

LETTER 3

Seek Me In The Garden Of Eden

My dearest child,

I love you very much. My love for you comes at a time when you feel isolated and alone in your journey and struggles. I am with you and will never leave your side despite the fact that at times you feel I have. I love you and care for you very deeply, to the point of dying for you personally so that you can experience life to the fullest; life the way it should be.

In your heart you truly know this deep down and I see your sadness and your hurt and pain, which you are suffering as I speak. Peace child, all will go well. I am carrying you through these turbulent times of uncertainty and sadness. You are special and mean a lot to me.

I see the ache in your heart of unfulfilled love and want you to look to me for total fulfilment.

I am the way and the bread of life. You shall be fulfilled and have your cup overflowing with joy and gladness. TRUST ME and look to me. I will fulfil all your desires and make your heart glad with rejoicing and you will sing aloud with joy and happiness, telling others what God has done for you. By this, many others shall come to know and see me through your loving example.

I am, and no one else can satisfy the hunger within you.

Please turn your time and attention to getting to know me. Try truly getting to know me in a deeper way and I shall bless your efforts abundantly. Take time out in your busy schedule, I will make a way for you each day when you can pray, meditate and study my Word. In this way you will be filled and satisfied and will no longer hunger or thirst.

I love you and desire a much closer relationship with you.

I want to teach you personally of my ways which lead to happiness and life. My way is the only way and I feel that you have finally stopped and are ready to hear the things I have so desperately wanted to tell you.

You have an open heart, an open mind and ears to hear.

I look forward to revealing my beautiful truth, grace, and mercy which will allow you to see the Father more clearly. In doing so you will grow bit by bit, changing and growing stronger day by day. My hand is upon you child, and I look forward to the beautiful days ahead as you are transformed inwardly; growing into that beautiful rose I intended you to be.

Take heart little child, don't be afraid. Be bold and walk where I have prepared the way.

Don't be frightened for I am with you every step of the way and care for you very much. Don't give up or become so easily discouraged, look to me for fulfilment and I will provide the necessary people around you to comfort, encourage and guide you as you walk with me in the Garden of Eden. Together we will walk down the path of life, teaching you as I live in you and you live in me. We shall walk hand in hand together sharing life's experiences as we grow closer and closer and become one.

This is the destiny that all men and women were created for: to be as one with their Creator, abounding in the beauty of life.

Look up; lift your eyes towards Heaven. Your Father is looking down at you and is pleased with your progress. He is overjoyed because you are listening with open ears, ready to hear all that he has to share with you. This indeed is a great day of rejoicing for us, the Father and me. You do not know how long we have waited for this day to come. We have so much to share with you and teach you. There is much to do and achieve together.

All can be done and achieved as long as you continue to have your eyes fixed towards Heaven; looking to us to fulfil your needs and desires. Your cup will overflow abundantly and your example will bring much healing and joy to those in similar circumstances. They will see the changes in your life and hear your testimony of heartfelt praise and rejoicing.

You are my humble servant, chosen by me since the beginning of time. I have set you apart for Holy use and will use your life and your walk to show others the way of life. The fruits born in your life will be evident and they will ask for what it is that you have.

I am well pleased with your efforts so far and have so much planned. No eye could see nor ear could hear what it is that I have planned for you and your family (1 Cor. 2:9). Your life will start to take on a dramatic difference and changes will be evident as you grow stronger and bolder in me, day-by-day.

You are a new creation and I now live the life within you that I have wanted to live within you ever since you were a little child.

How I have longed to show you the riches that lay ahead, but it wasn't until now that you had ears to hear and a heart and mind that truly sought after me. No more do I have to fight with other competing agendas; to be put back on the shelf or on the back burner. Now the fire is alive and will burn brighter than ever as you seek me wholeheartedly and unreservedly.

Come to my table, child and sing with the joy that I have placed in your heart. Tell your family of the wonderful works I am doing in your life. They will know that the Lord is involved and will be convicted by your words and heart. Rejoice I say, for the time has come. You truly are ready to hear the Words I long to share with you. As you obey and come to me, I shall feed and care for you, and together we shall be that light shining in a darkened world that knows no hope or love. Together we will overcome Satan and his evil ways which choke and destroy the earth and all its inhabitants.

Walk tall and be not afraid for I am in you and I have conquered Satan.

Go out little one and know that I am. Look towards God in Heaven. We will guide and direct your every step as you come to know us more personally and intimately. You will walk on water as you come to understand and believe all that we have planned for you. Just listen with an open heart and open ears.

Now go and rest, little child, and sleep well as you have a big day ahead tomorrow. I need you to be rested so that you can do the Lord's work on the Lord's day. Speak out praises and rejoice for the Lord is so happy and pleased that you have come to his Throne of grace to seek him and his ways. There is so much to tell you and so much to be accomplished.

So many are crying out for help to be shown the way to go. I will lead you to their side so you can comfort, encourage and love them wholeheartedly just as you have been loved by me. Tell them of the glory and the work that I have accomplished in your life. Tell those who mourn and cry out for help and healing of the fullness that now rests in your heart. Go and comfort my people, telling them of my good works that they too may seek me wholeheartedly just as you have done.

Rejoice and be glad for the day is coming when I shall wipe away every tear from their eye (Rev. 21:4) and personally comfort those who cry out for me. I shall fill them with my love through you and they shall know that it is I, the Lord, who has sent you to be my witness in their time of sadness and great need.

Go and I shall prepare a way for your little ones to be watched over, do not fret or worry for they are in my tender, loving care. You need not worry or be concerned about how you will do this or that, for these things shall be taken care of so that you can do the work of the Lord, to care for my little ones who are young in the faith and weak in heart.

I will give you the Words to speak and the courage to endure and be bold.

You need not be worried for the Spirit will show you which ones I want you to minister to. They shall be comforted and their burdens lifted as healing takes place in an amazing way. Suddenly they will begin to see me in a new light and will come to me personally through your example of love and forgiveness. In this way, many will rejoice in gladness as you help them to become one with me, just as you and I are one.

I am well-pleased and overjoyed little child, at your newfound love. I long to spend time with you to share the amazing grace of God and his love that surrounds us night and day.

Open your eyes to see the beauty that surrounds you, to the peace and tranquillity of the Garden of Eden. Sometimes you are unaware of the beauty that surrounds you, due to the anxieties of your heart and mind. Open your eyes and glimpse the glory that waits for your taking.

Come, eat of his fruit of the Tree of life, so that you may eat it and LIVE and tell of his greatness and blessings unmeasured that surround you night and day.

I have chosen you along with many others to re-enter the Garden to eat of the fruit. I long for you to enjoy and understand the great riches of mercy and grace that God has to offer each one of us; those that have ears to hear and eyes to see.

Go little one, I see that you are tired now from all the excitement and I long to be with you and tell you more every day as you seek me in the Garden of Eden. The richness and fullness of God's blessings are there for the taking, and it is his good pleasure to give them to you. Rejoice and be glad as the Heavens anticipate the day of my return. My Father will bestow you with fullness, as you do his will through me.

Rejoice and be glad for the time is coming when you will hear about miraculous healings and mighty conversions as God's Spirit moves, baptising all who desire to know him more deeply and intimately. People will be convicted in their hearts and will change as I come to live within them, leading them down the path of life, forgiveness, mercy and grace.

You are specially chosen for your merciful heart and I have given you the love you so desperately longed for as a child. Now you have been filled. Now you have been untapped to allow this great reservoir of love to flow through your heart and into the hearts of others as they come to know me in a beautiful fresh way. Although they had previously thought they knew me, they shall see me in a different light as if for the very first time.

The love that I have given you, I give you unreservedly.

Take this love and comfort to my little ones, bringing much joy to their hearts and healing to their souls. You are tired. I shall comfort and strengthen you so that you can do the work I have prepared for you.

Love them, hold them and restore the hope in their heart that they so desperately desire.

Shabbat Shalom

—— LETTER 4 ——

Without Love You Become As Nothing

My dearest little child,

    I am here beside you watching you as you write the Words that I give to you. I see you closing your eyes and I am standing beside you. Read 1 Corinthians 12 and I shall show you the Words you need to hear.

    Read I Corinthians 13 about faith, hope and love. Of these three, love is the greatest. Without love you become as nothing, a sounding brass or tinkling cymbal, a useless instrument in my possession. Never lose sight of this very important point.

    I cannot use you unless you have God's love flowing through you.

    You cannot do God's work unless you show love, one to

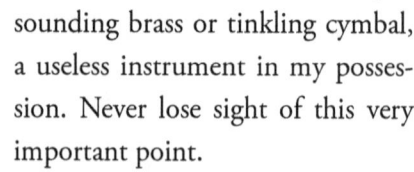

another, *with my love flowing through you.* By this they shall come to know the Father who sent me. Take heart little child, I shall send them to you to touch their heart and allow them to see the new light that shines within you.

Grace, peace and mercy I leave with you, until we walk in the Garden of Eden again.

Shabbat Shalom

LETTER 5

I Am The Resurrected Christ

My dearest child,

How I have longed to tell you all that is on my heart to share with those that I send to you. Believe and be not ashamed for I am with you in Spirit and in truth. The Words I speak to you are life and life much more abundantly.

Just as I came to the apostles after my death and resurrection, so too will I come to you and those who believe in me as the Anointed One. I will come to those who drink of my blood, eat of my flesh and proclaim of my coming; to those who seek earnestly to know me.

I am here right now in Spirit, protecting and guiding you as you write these Words in your journal. I am well pleased with your efforts and see the urgency in your heart for all those who mourn and seek after me.

I am the resurrected Christ who has risen so that you may have everlasting life with my Father and I in the Kingdom.

I am the resurrected Christ who gave up his glorious position in Heaven to live here on earth as a human man. I did this so that I could better understand all that you go through; so I could be your comforter when you are in pain or hurting; so I could know and understand the trials and tribulations that you go through.

I am the resurrected Christ who has come to bring many sons and daughters to glory. I am bringing them into the knowledge of God and his salvation through grace, mercy and faith in his resurrected son.

I am the resurrected Christ who died so that all may live and see me in an amazingly personal, new light. So that I may live within their hearts and they may live within me.

I have called you at this time to tell others of this Good News. I am calling you at this time to teach them through the *Alpha & Omega Board Game*®, so they may see me face-to-face as I reveal myself to them. Their hearts will be touched in a powerful and mighty way, and together with the Holy Spirit, they will be converted and brought back through the blood of the Lamb.

Rose of Sharon, you shall be the one to construct this board game to bring many sons and daughters to glory. I shall tell you how to play and the rules involved.

I am sending you to take this message around the world to teach them the way through my love which flows out like the waters cover the sea. The transformation of new life will be witnessed and preached to all peoples and nations, teaching many about the way to Eternal life.

You are to be my witness to the world. I want you to incorporate my teachings into the board game as I lead and guide you step-by-step. Do not fear little child, I will hold your hand and lead you gently. People will come to know me in a new light and new understanding; as if seeing me for the very first time. Then they will know God and see him as he really is, in all his power and majesty.

Yes this is an exciting and most blessed time. Who can know the fullness of my love and the healing that will come to those who cry out to know me? I am here right now by your side, instructing you as you write these Words. There is so much to do and achieve and so little time to prepare for what lies ahead.

Don't give up or become overwhelmed, my child. Rest in me and I shall lead you step-by-step in all that I have prepared for you. I will be with you, guiding you night and day as you complete the board game. True, I did come to you some time ago to plant the seed and I have been watering it and watching it grow while you have changed and developed. You, Rose of Sharon, have come to know me through my servants, whom I ordained as mentors for you, leading you into new understanding as I have lead them.

Yes, it is I, the Lord and not yourself who writes these Words.

Believe with your mind as you do in your heart the Words I am giving you. I am well pleased with you and look forward to instructing you more as we walk in the spiritual Garden of Eden, together again.

Shabbat Shalom

LETTER 6

Little By Little You Become Christ-Like

My dearest child,

I am with you always, carrying you through these turbulent times which you are now going through. This is to enable you to produce much fruit, and to lead many sons and daughters to my Father's Throne. Believe me when I say that I am with you right now and I see your head in your hands and feel your tiredness.

I am here by your side, always ready and willing to take your hand and guide you every step of the way which you need to walk. I am here, leading and guiding you so that you can accomplish all that I have planned for you. I have much to tell you and explain to you. I am excited to see that you truly do have ears to hear despite your busy life.

I want to share with you my plan for mankind as it was instigated in the beginning with Adam and Eve, where they too walked with me in the Garden of Eden as you are doing now.

I have created mankind for a purpose here on earth.

Every person shall come to know me as their personal Saviour and have an intimate and close relationship as I reveal myself to them. Fear not little child, for I am here and shall lead and guide you every step of the way. You shall never feel abandoned or alone as I live my life within you and you live your life within me. This is indeed a very difficult concept to grasp with your mind.

I live within you as you drink in my Words and allow your heart to be renewed and transformed.

Your heart will be softened by my Holy Spirit allowing me to mould and shape your character. My Spirit that I pour into you will blend with your human Spirit and thus little by little you become Christ-like.

This is difficult for you to understand but I know that you are being changed as you allow my goodness to flow through you. I have called you to lead my people out of darkness into a renewed relationship with me; involving their hearts and not just their minds.

As they truly search for me with their hearts, I will work within them to change their stony hearts to pliable clay (Ez. 11:19).

I will shape them with the Holy Spirit which I will send in abundance. As they ask for their cup to be filled, so shall I fill it to overflowing.

Take heart and rejoice little child, I see the difficulties you are facing. I am here and will work with you at the pace you are able. Just as the rain softens the earth outside your window, so I shall soften the hearts of those who seek me wholeheartedly and without reservation.

I hear your question regarding how it is that you live within me. It is through your spiritual essence that you live in my heart. In this way we are truly ONE body and ONE Spirit; ONE church and ONE temple made Holy and ready for my return, when I restore God's glory here on earth.

The prayers of my people are heard and I come quickly to restore order amongst the chaos that pervades the earth ruled by Satan and his demons. They have dominion at present but cannot affect those that I have set apart by my hand for a special purpose and calling.

The time is coming very soon when my people shall hear my voice, for my sheep know the voice of their Shepherd. The time is coming very soon when my people will call out to me and I shall answer their call to know me in a new and different light.

You are my chosen one in whom I am well pleased; I see your efforts and see the desire of your heart to please me. You are indeed doing God's work as I desire.

Please comfort your brothers and sisters, with open arms and an open heart. Let them experience the love that flows through you and into those I am calling to myself. They are hurting and need unconditional love and prayer for healing and they have begun their journey in seeking to find me.

I shall not keep you too long as I know that you do not want to stay up too late at night but I want to share with you how much your faith and obedience will enable many to come to see me in a new and more personal way.

I am sending you my servants to administer to your needs and they will show you the way in which I want you to go. I have placed them by your side to help you grow and develop. They will help bring you yet closer to my side. It is my great joy that you have come to this point in your life and I am glad to see the happiness in your heart as you discover the gifts God has showered upon you for his work and his glory.

There is much to be accomplished but it shall be done in God's magnificent timing. Go and sleep my child, rest and be refreshed for our walk again tomorrow, for I long to teach you more of my ways. Rejoice and sing for the joy that now dwells in your heart, for this also is a gift from God.

Shabbat Shalom

LETTER 7

Alpha & Omega Board Game® Revealed

My Dearest Rose of Sharon

I have awoken you from your sleep to tell you of the rules of the Game which I wish you to complete for me. I am just as excited about the completion of this game as you are anxious to have it totally completed. I see the smile on your face and in your heart as that day draws near to completion.

My game is to bring many sons and daughters to glory and it is to show them how they can develop a close and personal and intimate relationship with myself and God the Father through utilizing the Holy Spirit in all its fullness and power to draw many to his wonderful and most Holy Throne of grace.

My game is to be called *Alpha & Omega Board Game*® since it is to represent coming to know me from beginning to the end. I am the Anointed one, Holy and righteous Lamb of God, Saviour for all mankind. To this end I was born part God, part man, in order to take on all mankind's sins and allow them to stand before God.

I became sin and was sacrificed so that all who believe could have direct access to God the Father and know him as Lord God and the love he shines upon all those that seek to find him face-to-face.

I will now give you the rules for *Alpha & Omega* as I want you to type them out for all to read during the gameplay and in doing so, shall know that this game was written by me. Fear not little child, you don't have to worry, just merely listen and obey my directions.

Shabbat Shalom

Alpha & Omega Rules Overview

This game is to be played by 2-4 people and it is a self-discovery game which enables anyone to come to know Jesus Christ, who is the Alpha & Omega. Each player begins by choosing to have a relationship with Jesus Christ. This is the desire of the Alpha & Omega to come to know all those who seek him with their open heart.

Each player begins on the colour of their choice and this represents them coming to Jesus Christ through accepting his crucifixion and resurrection and thus they are baptised into being a new creation, represented by a butterfly.

Now their journey can begin as they develop their relationship with Jesus Christ, or they can choose to develop the fruits of the Holy Spirit. Your game goals are of developing a relationship with Jesus Christ, removing barriers, receiving fruits of the Holy Spirit and adjusting an attitude.

Once you have the required fruits of the Holy Spirit, have developed a relationship with Jesus Christ and have obtained a positive attitude, you are then able to approach God's Throne of grace through Jesus Christ's sacrifice, your sins have been atoned and you have been made white as snow, enabling you to approach God's Heavenly Throne of grace.

It is through God's forgiveness, grace, mercy and incredible love that we are able to enter his most Holy of Holies. It is here that we have been destined to come and sit at the Father's feet to be taught of his ways and to receive the Heavenly gifts he so very much wants to shower down upon us.

This is so every one of us are able to come to know him as our own personal Father, just as Christ knew him as his very own Father.

For we are his adopted sons and daughters called to become part of his body and Holy temple. Each one of us builds up and edifies each other in order to create that beautiful Holy temple of people to worship and praise his name, and to be glorified at Jesus Christ's second coming. Then we shall see him in his glory and majesty that the Father has bestowed upon him.

Indeed he is Alpha and Omega, the beginning and the end and all who are being called now are to become as he is and was and is to be. We become transformed and changed through the power of the Holy Spirit and we become as Christ, as we live in Christ, and Christ lives in us. Together we shall be glorified at his second coming as we rise to meet him in the air, and so we shall be transformed from our earthly bodies and become one in the fullness of the glory that surrounds Heaven.

It is for this end that we were born; thus for a little while our earthly bodies are subject to the cares and worries of this world, but so too, just as we died and were resurrected as represented in baptism, so too we will rise and become a new spiritual creation. The inner man is being renewed day by day by the gift of God's Holy Spirit, yet the outward man is decaying.

Who can know the things that God has planned for those that seek to find Christ and seek to have a relationship with him and the Heavenly Father? It is only through Christ's sacrifice, death and resurrection that we are able to enter God's Holy Throne of grace. Here we can come to hear of his way and know and be touched personally by his incredible love. This enables us to be healed totally as we begin to forgive those who have sinned against us. We are cleansed of our sins by the blood of the Lamb, the testimony of God's love that he gave us in his only begotten son, so that we could have access to his Throne. We can then come to know him intimately as our Father, Abba, most Holy Heavenly One, who is Omnipotent and Almighty; the Majesty and King, whom all angels rejoice over, and bow down before his great and most Holy beautiful Throne.

All praises to God, our Heavenly Father who is and was and is to come. The Eternal Everlasting Father who longs to draw us to him so that he may reveal to us his most amazing love, joy, peace, kindness, goodness, gentleness, patience, self-control and faithfulness. These fruits of the Holy Spirit are gifts which the Father in Heaven longs to give to those who seek him and his way. These are given freely to those who accept Jesus Christ as their personal Saviour and begin their new life as a new creation in Christ.

This allows us to become as Christ and so we begin to see the Father in Spirit and all that come to him must come to him in Spirit to worship and praise him for his name's sake. (Eph. 2:18 & John 4:24)

For everyone who enters the Holy of Holies must bow down as they are in his very presence. In this way we enter his Throne of grace through the Spirit, and so we worship him and sing praises and rejoice for he is Spirit and all who worship him come to him in the Spirit.

In this way our inner Spirit is being renewed day by day as we partake of his Holy Spirit, enabling us to be recreated by the potter into a new vessel for his use and we will then fit together to create a perfected Heavenly temple, as he draws and recreates each one to become a new creation in Christ (2 Cor. 5:17).

Prayer

Arise and you shall see the Lord of Hosts as your Heavenly Father that sits upon his most Holy Throne in a new and different way. You will have access to him through his only begotten son who died so that we could stand in his place and come to know God the Father and be transformed from this earthly body into a new Heavenly spiritual body that is perfectly fashioned in every way and without spot, blemish or wrinkle, fitting together with other sons and daughters in perfect unity as we become as *one through God's glorious Heavenly Spirit – This indeed is the ALPHA and OMEGA.*

Shabbat Shalom

LETTER 8

Proclaim The Lord's Will In Your life

My dearest child,

I see your pain and heartache and know the desires of your heart. I am with you my child, carrying you through this sad time. I know your heart and the desires you have and how much you long for healing and release in these areas of your life. Take heart little child, I am with you right by your side leading you through this troubled time.

I love you and died for you so you can place your worries and cares at my feet and be free to do my work which I need you to do.

I see your troubled heart and long to help you through this turbulent time. Trust in me and I will guide you every step of the way, teaching you what to do in each circumstance.

You must proclaim the Lord's will in your life because you are a new creation in Christ and I now live within your heart.

I am there to care, comfort and console you during troubled times. My love for you is strong and I long for you to look to me for all your answers. I will care for you my child. I will rescue you. I will be there for you night and day, just call out for me and I'll be there at your side. Don't give up in your heart. Be strong and follow me. Care for my little ones who need nurturing and I shall put it upon your heart what to say and then they shall know it is from God.

Take heart little one, I see your sadness and confusion, but all will go well and all will become clear as you begin to see the unveiling of my master plan.

I am by your side to guide and strengthen you so that you can accomplish all that I have planned for you.

I know your heart and your desires. I see your pain and anguish regarding your family members. All is not lost; I am bringing them to that place that you so long for them to be. In my timing I will bring them to that place of rest and peace. Fear not little child, take heart; my love for them is stronger than yours. I died so they too, could experience life.

Cheer up and don't let Satan steal away your joy for this doesn't achieve the Father's will. The Father longs for you to be happy and joyful in order to bring many out of darkness and into his glorious light.

Be strong and fear not, I shall be that hope that you so much desire in your heart. Look to me and I shall strengthen you in this troubled time. Be at peace my child; all will go well. My will is being done here on earth as we speak.

Don't look at troubling events and become concerned, my hand is upon these things and all you have to do is look to me continually for strength to endure to the end. Don't fear or be afraid for my hand is upon you. There are major events about to explode and much is to be accomplished, but God's will is being done as I speak.

My servants across the world are now preparing for my second coming and I am preparing the hearts of my people.

They will truly have a thirst and a yearning to come to know me and I will reveal myself to them as they seek to find my face. I will reveal to them my true identity and they will have the same intimate relationship you do.

There will be strong opposition against the works you are about to do.

Know that I am the Lord who has called you personally and set you apart for a special calling at this time. I have prepared a special job which I need you to do in order to proclaim the Lord and his second coming.

Take heart and be not afraid child, I am with you and will never leave your side. Call on me when you need me. I am here by your side holding your hand and leading you where I want you to go.

Shabbat Shalom

LETTER 9

Anointed One Who Died For You

Dearest child,

My love for you cannot be compared with those that surround you who do not understand the great price that was paid to purchase your soul. My love for you is so immense that you cannot even begin to understand or fathom the height or depth or width of my love (Rom. 8:39).

Your love for me comes from an understanding of my love for you.

I am here by your side ready to take your hand to teach you all that I long to share with you of the beauty that the Father has for those who truly love him and seek his ways.

I am the Anointed One who died for you personally to show you just how much I truly do love you.

I care for you so much more than you will ever know and I love your family with the same love and affection and I will not allow them to be hurt in any way.

I want to tell you now about why it is that I allow you to suffer these things that you are now suffering and why your heart is weighed down with such heaviness and sadness. You see so many around you searching and seeking after me, yet not coming to know me as you have done.

I see their heart and know their ways and desires and long to show myself to them, but they do not know how or in which way they can come to see me.

This is where I'm calling you to show them the way so that they can see me face-to-face. I desire for them to see the Father in such a new light and new understanding that they too can be as happy and joyous in truly coming to know me personally and intimately.

I have chosen you as my special vessel to teach those around you of this exciting and new way of life so that they also can share in God's glory and love which fills those who seek him whole-heartedly, without reservation.

I am the Lord, the Almighty King who died and rose again to Eternal, everlasting life.

I am the Lord, the everlasting omnipotent King who reigns at the right hand of God and will return in full power and authority in the glory that my Father will bestow upon me. I long to reveal myself to those who seek to come to know me and they shall see me and know that I am the Lord whom they seek. I will reveal myself to those who truly have ears to hear, as you have finally reached this point.

I want you to tell your story to those whom I send to you, who ask of the hope that lies within. Through your testimony and gifting you will show many the ways in which they may come to see me in a new light. Well done good and faithful servant. I am well pleased with what you have done so far and see your desire to show many the way. Say to them what I stir within you to say, for this shall be the witness that will guide them to me and the Father.

It is indeed a most exciting time and you have been chosen as an instrument in bringing my lost Lambs back to me. Show them the love that I have for you and for all who seek me, and they too shall experience the same healing and joy which you have come to experience in me. You are my chosen one whom I love and care for very much. Be of good cheer and sing praises and rejoice, for a new time is about to take place when many will come to truly know me as they have never known me before.

Much healing will occur in their hearts as I break them and remake them with my love and my Spirit which I place within them.

I have longed for this since the beginning of creation and now this new and exciting time is about to take place. The Heavens groan in anticipation of this coming time, as one by one my children come to know me and the Father in a deeply personal way.

My love for you is such that I shall protect you and provide for your needs as you do the work that I have chosen you to do.

It is with great anticipation and excitement that we wait to see the hearts of those whom we love so dearly and who love us also come to see us as you do. Praise and rejoice with us as we watch more lives being changed and hearts renewed, growing day by day as God's Spirit changes them into new creations.

Your life is about to take flight and blossom into the beautiful rose I have desired for you to become. My love has been the food and nourishment to enable you to develop into the rose you will become.

Arise my darling, come with me and you shall know that it is I, your Lord, who waits patiently for you, who longs to show you the riches and the glory God so eagerly waits to share with you and all those he is calling at this time. I love you and will never leave you nor forsake you.

Take heart little child, I am here by your side leading you constantly day and night and carrying you as you need me to.

Shabbat Shalom

LETTER 10

Enter And Sit At The Father's Feet

My dearest child,

I was saddened to hear that you initially didn't want me to wake you up because of fear.

I am always with you by your side and shall lead you gently in the path I would like you to walk down. It is entirely your decision as to whether you choose to go down this path where I am taking you.

Please know that I shall indeed carry you during the times when you need me to and know that there is much I long to tell you. I am giving you my peace, safety and security, placing my angels around you so that you need not fear anything from the evil one.

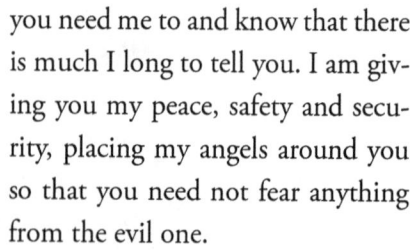

My hand is upon you and your family, to allow you to do my work with safe assurance.

My love for you cannot be compared to anything of human origin. Just know and believe that I indeed love you very deeply and will never allow anything to harm you in any way. You are being watched over and strengthened to allow you to carry out the work that I have set for you to complete.

I am excited about the new love that many will come to display as their hearts are turned towards the Father. I am excited for the new relationships that will be developed and nurtured by my people as they gather together for my name's sake.

Praise to God the Father who sits on his Throne in Heaven looking upon the earth and all those on it who seek after him with earnestness and sincerity. He longs to teach men and women about his grace and the opportunity they have to approach the Holy of Holies through my atoning sacrifice.

I am the Lord God who died so that you may enter and sit at the Father's feet, to learn all that he wants to share with you. Go and teach others of this newfound information and revelation which I, the Lord Jesus Christ, have personally given to you so that you may share this Gospel of the Good News with all that come into contact with you.

My hand is upon the *Alpha & Omega Board Game*® and I shall guide you step-by-step as you develop and perfect it for my name's sake. Be bold and proclaim my name to those who you come into contact with so that they also may come to know me as you have.

I long to receive the love that many have in their hearts for me, but who do not know how to enter into the Holy of Holies to worship in Spirit and in truth forever, Amen.

Prayer

Oh most high God and Father, we kneel before your Heavenly Throne, please lead us to where you want us to go in order for us to praise and honour and worship you with all our heart and mind and soul. We long to come to know you Heavenly Father as Jesus Christ knows you, and we long to be in your very presence, that you may teach us of your ways in which we wish to go.

Please lead and guide us. Take us to that place of peace and safety where we can indeed rest in your arms and know that your hand is upon us and you are guiding us to come to know you more personally and much more intimately. We long to hear your voice when you call out to us so we can answer your call, and we can arise to be with you in Spirit to worship and praise your most Holy name.

We offer our lives as living sacrifices so that we can become that perfect and Holy temple, unified and knitted together in perfect harmony. Cleanse us oh Lord of our sins, and transform our earthly bodies into a beautiful new vessel that you can use to bring honour and glory for your name's sake, so that all mankind may come to know you in this way. Praise and rejoice for the Lord has come and made a way for all mankind to approach the Heavenly Father in Spirit and in truth.

Praise and rejoice for he is the King of Kings and Lord of Lords and greatly to be praised by all mankind as they come to know him as their Lord and Saviour. Who was, and is, and is to come. He is the Alpha and Omega, the beginning and the end. For our righteousness sake, he came to earth to endure the cross set before him.

He, who knew no sin, died on the cross, in order to bring many to God's glorious Throne, in order for them to be sanctified, set apart, and made as white as snow, spotless and without blemish or wrinkle, perfect in the eyes of God; so he could have a direct relationship with all those who call upon his name in praise and worship.

This is indeed the very reason why Christ entered into the world as a human child, in order to know and understand what it was like to be human and to suffer; to become our high Priest and intercessor. As a result we can cry out to him anytime, day or night, and ask for his divine help and intervention as he intercedes for us before the Father.

We have been given an opportunity to be renewed inwardly every day as we partake of God's gift; his most precious Holy Spirit and his Holy Word as written in the Bible. In this way we become a new creation in Christ, citizens of his spiritual Kingdom, and guaranteed Eternal life at Jesus Christ's second coming when his glory and majesty shall be revealed for all mankind to witness. That great and glorious day of the Lord will soon be upon us and the whole earth waits and groans in anticipation for it.

Much rejoicing will occur when we are at last caught up in the air with Christ our Saviour and King and our earthly bodies are transformed to resemble Christ in all his glory. Together we shall form that perfectly unified temple which God is now building with his hands. Amen.

Shabbat Shalom

LETTER 11

Show You New Revelations

My dearest child,

I have longed to talk with you to tell you of the plans I have for the *Alpha & Omega Board Game®* and how I will use it as a tool to bring many to know me, and the immense love that I have for all mankind.

You are so young in heart and so easily swayed. Beware, the lion is lurking and seeking to devour the innocent who are so easily deceived. Stay close to me and I will give you the petitions of your heart. You will know when I am calling you. Take heart. Be strong. Know that I am and I have given you this gift in order to help those that need God's message of love to encourage and guide them back to him.

Come, let us rejoice and sing praises to God for his most generous mercy and love.

Know that he has all things in Heaven and in earth under control. We long to see him in all his glory on that great and wonderful day of the Lord. At my return you shall be changed, in the twinkling of an eye, you shall become as I am (1Cor. 15:52). I am going to show you new revelations and enable you to reveal them to those you come into contact with; to build up and edify. In doing so we will create that perfectly unified temple.

My love for you is such that I endured the pain on the cross so that you could experience life and Heavenly gifts that God so desperately desires to give you and others who seek to know him.

I am doing a mighty work in this end time and will do it through the vessels which I am now preparing and making ready. My hand is upon you my child and I long to teach you much about the love that God has for all who seek him with all their heart, mind and soul. Be of good cheer and replenish the hope that lies within so that you can give an answer to anyone who inquires.

Take care my child, be not overcome with sadness and grief, but dance and sing for the joy of the Lord is upon you. Let all see the love that you have received from the Father and me, in order to bring glory to God and lead many to his table of thanksgiving and singing.

Shabbat Shalom

LETTER 12

Be Open To Hearing My Spirit

My dearest child,

My presence is made known to you through these writings and I abide within you and you abide within me. Your love for me draws me closer to you and together we are joined to do the work that God has ordained for us to do.

Be of good cheer my child; persevere with my readings, so that you will be filled with God's Holy Spirit, which will then enable you to finish the work of the game.

I have chosen you to create the *Alpha & Omega Board Game*® and I am with you in Spirit every step of the way. I am well pleased with what you have completed and it will be used as a mighty tool to draw many to God the Father and myself, the crucified one.

I am here right now to guide and lead you. Be open to hearing my Spirit so that all may be accomplished for my name's sake. Satan can have no part in it. He is bound up and cannot have any part in what I am doing through you.

Be still my child and be at peace. My hand is upon you and my Father's will is being done in order to glorify God the Father, the Omnipotent and Almighty One, who reigns supreme in Heaven above. Thoughts will come to you today that I would like you to put into action in order to complete the game so that it is ready to be played by those who are being called at this time.

Rejoice my child and be of good cheer for I have overcome the evil one and he will be cast down and trodden underfoot as we rise to meet God at his glorious Heavenly Throne. Triumphantly we sing aloud and praise God's Holy name among his people as we become transformed and renewed through his grace and mercy.

Be still my child and know that I have come and died so that you may experience life and a personal relationship with God the Father.

Shabbat Shalom

LETTER 13

I Was Willing To Die In Your Stead

My dearest child,

I love and care for you very much, and as such would like to show you what I have planned for you and your family. My love for you spurred me to endure much hardship and pain as I died on the cross for your personal benefit.

*Please take this gift of life that I give you to bring glory to God and his magnificent omnipotent Heavenly Throne room filled with cherubim, ser-*aphim and angels of every shape and description, all singing praises to God the most high.

My love for you is such that I was willing to die in your stead so that you could live and come to know me and the Heavenly Father, much deeper and closer. We both long for you to come to know us in the intimate relationship we have developed with you over time. We have watched you grow and develop over the years and have longed for the day when you were ready to hear all that we have planned for you to do and to become.

Thank you for your tireless efforts so far. I know how busy your lifestyle is, looking after your family. I am so proud of you, Rose of Sharon, for your determination throughout the years, for never giving up on completing the board game, always knowing that it was instigated by my Father and me. We too, long for the time when it is completed and played by those with hearts who seek to come and know us more closely.

Be of good cheer, at last this much awaited day has come and you shall know it is the appointed time for you to finish the game. The wait is over and now is the time to put the game together for publishing and printing. My hand is upon that also and I shall show you step-by-step what it is I want you to do.

Please listen carefully to the Words I have to tell you. It is of most importance my child.

Satan longs to devour my plan to allow men and women to have direct contact with myself and the Father, as he knows the harm it will do in destroying his cleverly disguised lies.

He knows the incredibly powerful tool that you hold and as such longs to devour it as well as you. Beware, don't listen to his lies but stay close to the Father and I as we teach you step-by-step. In this way he won't be able to get a foothold and destroy the work we have already begun in you.

We will open the doors that neither man nor Satan will be able to close, and close doors that neither man nor Satan will be able to open (Is. 22:22).

Our angels shall go before you to prepare the way and they shall know that you have been sent by us. The Spirit will show them that my hand is upon you, my child. Therefore be bold and speak out my name and the Father's name and his praise and glory to those around you. Be my witness and share your testimony to those I send to you.

Your love for me and the Father is strong and as such it will be a powerful testimony because they will feel you speaking from the heart. They will see and hear the conviction in your eyes and in your voice.

Never lose sight of your love for us and Satan won't be able to gain entry as he has previously.

So many times Satan had nearly taken your soul because you believed the clever lies he told you. Unaware, your life was slowly being devoured, until you allowed me to enter your heart. Slowly, over time I could reveal to you all of the lies and falsehoods that Satan had deceived you with, as he has and is doing with so many others.

It is for this very purpose that we urgently need you to shout out and tell others of your newfound life and also to complete the board game and free them from the lies and the hold that Satan has over their life. It is a race against time as I see so many hurting and in pain, crying out to me in their prayers, in need of a teacher to show them the way. We do indeed live in the end times and Satan knows he has but a short time to deal with those that are yet to be called for a Holy purpose.

Please join me in the crusade to announce to the world the incredible Good News of God's coming Kingdom which he so desperately desires to place in each of your hearts and minds.

You are renewed every day as you drink in his Word and the precious Holy Spirit. You are Holy, sanctified and set apart, and as such cannot be touched by Satan the devil. He is very clever, deceitful and crafty and knows your weaknesses. Beware, for he is continually prowling about, seeking whom he can devour and destroy (1 Peter 5:8).

Take heart little child, do not be afraid and don't let fear take over your mind for I shall protect and guide you, making you aware of the devices he uses to discourage and cut down your joy.

Be of good cheer for God sits in his Heavenly Throne, watching over all, to stay the hand of Satan when needed.

Be strong and be bold my child, my hand is upon you and I shall take you to places where I want you to speak openly of the things I have revealed to you, of your testimony, your life and the joy that you now know. I will prepare an abiding place for you to receive those I send so that you can teach them of my ways and of the love my Father and I have for all those who seek us.

Go now my child, Rose of Sharon, and sleep, as you have a very busy day ahead and I am excited at the prospect of seeing the completed game. Then you will be able to play it with those that I send to you whose hearts are open and willing to play. It truly is an exciting time. Tomorrow will happen as we have ordained it will happen.

Shabbat Shalom

LETTER 14

Heart For God

My dearest child,

Thank you for your obedience in writing this letter at this time. I shall reward you greatly by strengthening you tomorrow and in the days to come. My child, listen carefully to what it is I have to say to you.

My love is to be poured out to all those that seek me; who surrender and seek after me with an open, contrite and teachable heart. In this way they shall be filled to overflowing. They shall want no more, for the Shepherd will place love in their hearts and they shall know the Shepherd's voice whenever I speak to them in Spirit.

This is most precious to my heart and I long to pour out this love to those who are drawn to me at this time. Much sadness and loss will occur which will turn people's hearts back to me.

I shall then answer their call in full with the love that my Father has given to me.

In this manner, many people will be led back to God the Father and they shall know his incredible love, mercy, grace and forgiveness. It is for this reason that I came to earth to establish a group of people who would carry my message until the time of my return. Christ, the crucified one, will be thus proclaimed, leading many to a greater understanding.

I am extremely excited with the prospect of so many coming to know myself and God. Miraculous healing will occur in order to bring glory to God and proclaim his name among the people. I have chosen to work with you now ahead of time to prepare and instruct them in the way they should go. For how will they know unless I send a teacher to teach them of my ways?

This is indeed a most exciting time which will unfold very soon as I bring various people to play the *Alpha & Omega Board Game®*. I shall make a way for them to play according to my plan. Take heart little child and be of good cheer. Don't allow the evil one to steal away your joy and gladness. He seeks to devour your soul. Stay close to me for I shall guard you day and night. Be bold and walk uprightly, for I am here by your side to lead and guide you as you complete the final stages of the game.

My love for you is great; never forget that I died so that you could be freed from the penalty of death.

The life you now lead, you lead in me. I shall guide you to the church I wish you to attend regularly. I will prepare the way so that you will be able to be fed spiritually and God will be glorified in full. Praise and rejoice for God is good! Know that he has made all things in Heaven and earth through me. As I listened, I did all that he said.

Likewise I would like you also to listen and obey as I teach you these things. In this way you will be used as a powerful tool to show God's light which will shine in your eyes and be shown through your deeds. Be still my child. Do not worry, I shall wake you to write more as I require. Sleep and be refreshed for tomorrow.

Shabbat Shalom

LETTER 15

I Am Here In Spirit

My dearest child,

You are my precious child and I have set you apart to feed my flock with the Words I give to you. These Words are life and will refresh the souls who hear them spoken out loud. My love grows stronger for those who cry out from the flock to be fed and nourished.

I am life and they must eat my body and drink my blood (John 6:56) in order to see my face and hear my voice. I will come to nurture my church, the body of people who know my voice when I speak. They will be gathered together to be safely guarded, fed and nurtured. There will be much gladness and rejoicing when this long-awaited time has arrived.

My dearest child I see your heart and how you have been yearning for this time to come. It will indeed come and there will be tears of joy as many will be delivered and offered up to God the Father and myself.

They shall offer themselves to do the work of God in bringing many sons and daughters into this new understanding which I now give to you.

Carry this message to my people around the world as they come to know me. I will teach them of my way personally, as they believe and listen to all that I tell them. Be still my child and know that it is I, Jesus Christ, who lives within you and teaches you the things you are now writing down.

Celebrate and shout aloud as I am here on earth now moving in a mighty way through my people. I am here in Spirit and I am working through the hearts of those who know my voice when I call aloud to them. My love will go out before me and heal those who cry out for healing and release.

I am here in Spirit to live amongst my people; to teach them of my love and sacrifice in order to bring them to the Father's Throne of grace. My Father longs to know each one personally and develop a relationship as he teaches them the way in which he wants them to go. He longs for each one to know and love him; to see him and experience the love and spiritual gifts he longs to give to all who come to him.

I am here in Spirit and moving amongst my people, revealing and showing myself as they seek to find me. As they draw near to me, I will draw near to them (Jam. 4:8).

This is indeed a very joyous time as I live within the hearts of my people and move upon the earth in a mighty way, opening up the minds and hearts of those who will come to see me clearly for the first time. They shall truly know me as never before.

I will be their God and they shall be my people (Jer. 32:38). They will know my voice when I call aloud. They will obey and offer up their lives as living sacrifices in order to allow me to achieve all that

I need to in this end time. Take heart my child, fear not, be of good cheer and sing your praises to God for the good things that he is accomplishing in your life. Shout aloud and rejoice for you are a child of God and set apart to do my work as I reveal it to you.

Shabbat Shalom

LETTER 16

Hope And Glory

My loving child,

I require your attention to listen to the Words I have to say. I chose you to bring about the changes I am putting in place as my Word goes forth into the world. I will open the hearts and minds of those whom I am calling at this time and they shall hear my voice, and they shall be my people. I am excited for my Word to be widespread for healing to occur. The Spirit yearns as it waits in readiness to prepare my people for my imminent return.

Fear not, little child, I will be your rock and salvation, and shall strengthen you in all that you do. My hand is upon you and I am guiding you in the path in which you shall go. Spread the news as you go where I send you. Reveal to others the hope and glory that lies within you, praising God's glorious name forever, Amen.

Prayer

Give us this day, our daily bread.
Forgive us our iniquities.
Shine forth your glory, majesty and honour,
as Jesus Christ is being revealed in us as a new creation
and new being under Heaven.
Forgive us our sins as we forgive others.
Lead us not into temptation but deliver us from the evil one
who lurks around like a lion anxious to devour.
Believe in Jesus Christ, the Anointed One who died so that we can
have life so much more abundantly. Remember our sins no more,
as far as the east is from the west. As each day passes our love
grows for Jesus and we offer up ourselves as living sacrifices
for his glory, honour and worship forever. Amen.

Thank you for your obedience and love, my child. Be still and know that I am the Lord God.

Shabbat Shalom

LETTER 17

Remember Your Creator

My dearest child,

Your love is beginning to flourish as you walk in my ways and listen to the Words that I speak.

At times you have disobeyed my voice and heeded the consequences. Much sadness and suffering could have been avoided but I was able to carry you through these times.

Be still my child and know that I am the Lord, the Anointed One, who can heal all peoples. Know that the fruit that will be produced as a result of sickness will be good. It will draw the hearts together and bring them to the point where I can teach them of the ways in which I want them to go.

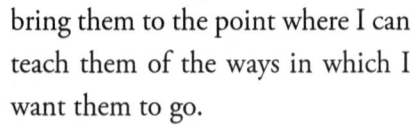

Remember your Creator in the days of your youth, for you may need to call upon him in your later years. I have come to give life much more abundantly. One by one they shall be led unto me to renew their relationship and understanding as I call them all by name. This was predestined from the beginning.

Be of good cheer my child and renew the hope that lies within you. Await my return to earth when I will show my strength, power and glory for all nations to see. Behold I come quickly, as a thief in the night ready to change those who hear my voice into spiritual beings.

Indeed the time draws near and my presence fills the earth in the hearts and minds of all those that search me out. They shall find me as never before and I will reveal myself to them in a new and exciting way. This time shall be a time of great rejoicing and many hearts will be convicted and changed in the near future.

I am now preparing the way for my people to have ears to hear and eyes to see the coming of the Lord. Yes, I will first live in the hearts and minds of men and women as my work is accomplished through them. Then I will later manifest myself in the full glory and honour given to me by my Father in Heaven, at my second coming.

My work is being accomplished here on earth right now through various forms and ways; all glorifying our Father and his Heavenly Throne. All praise belongs to him.

Prayer

Oh Heavenly Father, whom we love and adore,
you are our Creator who sustains us upon this earth.
Without you we would not maintain our existence here on earth.
Your love for us is so precious,
who can fathom the depth and richness of your mercy and grace?
Your love for us is such that you allowed your only begotten son to die,
so that we may have life and life much more abundantly.
You knew each one of us before we were conceived

and have watched us grow and change over the years.
Your love for us is incomprehensible,
and we do not understand the reason for your endless love, grace and mercy.
Your love never ends and washes over us to cleanse us.
You make us new by the blood of the most precious Lamb of God.
You are our God and we are your people.
Our hearts now turn to you, oh God, and
we ask for your mercy, grace, love and forgiveness.
Only then can we be at peace as one.
Only then can we truly see your face and know your voice.
Our hearts cry out to you, oh Father God.
Please do not turn away from us and cut us off again,
but open the gates of Eden to allow all to enter into
this precious relationship with you and your son, Jesus Christ.
Amen

Shabbat Shalom

LETTER 18

My Master Plan For Mankind

My precious child,

I am writing through you to announce my master plan for mankind. I am calling each individual and personally revealing myself to them, convicting them within their heart.

They can either accept or reject my calling upon their life as they seek to come to know me with their whole heart, mind and soul.

I will be found by those who seek me and many will be converted at this time. It is a most wondrous time indeed as they turn from their selfish ways and begin to praise God the Father in his Heavenly Throne. They will develop this relationship with God the Father; he shall be their God and they shall be his people.

Much healing shall occur as hearts are renewed and I will place my Spirit within them, which will combine with their human Spirit.

My love will then flow out upon the nation through those whom I have prepared to receive it and they will show forth God's glory upon the earth as it is now in Heaven. Many sons and daughters shall know the Father and I, praising and rejoicing aloud of the love that reigns upon the earth. He has heard their cry and answered their call for help and deliverance from the evil one.

God's love will flow openly for a time, until his purpose is accomplished. My heart yearns for that time which is about to take place as I prepare my temple of living sacrifices; the hearts given to God the Father.

My love will conquer the immense sadness and hopelessness that now fills the earth. My people shall hear the Shepherd's voice and I shall gather all my sheep together and feed them in green pastures beside still waters.

They will be fed and they will go out to preach the Good News to those around them. Many shall come to know God and shall be saved through the blood of Jesus Christ, the crucified and Anointed One. It is for this purpose that he came to earth, so that many could be saved and come to know God the Father. Amen.

Please pass this message on to those whom I inspire you to show. My Word shall go forth into all the nations and many shall hear and obey and come into an intimate relationship with myself and the Father.

This is indeed exciting times and my love shall go forth and conquer the hatred, anger and sadness that fills the earth. Many who are hurting will be healed and they shall be released from the chains of bondage as my Word goes out to my people.

Shabbat Shalom

LETTER 19

Perfect In His Eyes

My dearest child,

I have called you at this time to reveal my truth. I love you and died for you so that you may experience the forgiveness of your sins; to be remembered no more. You are as a perfect rose in my Father's eyes as he looks upon your countenance. He sees you without spot or blemish, Holy and set apart to be used by him to do his work.

He has called you by name and chosen you to do a mighty work in witnessing to the nations in the form of the *Alpha & Omega Board Game*. I am nothing without my Father, and the reason for my being is to be a personal Saviour to those that seek God, allowing them to be sanctified and have access to God the Father and his Heavenly Throne. The Holy Spirit is sent to grow and develop those who are being called as they come to know the Father and me.

The Holy Spirit strengthens the weak, heals the sick and delivers those from temptation who cry out from the depths of darkness. The Holy Spirit helps to renew their heart and mind as they are transformed and set apart; Holy in the eyes of God the Father.

God sees them as they will be, when glorified at my return. A relationship is required as they draw closer to the Father through a better understanding of who I am and why I needed to die in order that they might live and live abundantly.

My love for my people is such that the Holy Spirit will live within them and they shall live within me. Together we will form that perfectly unified Holy temple to bring glory to God.

All praise belongs to God the Father, who is greatly to be praised. My love for you is vast and your obedience to writing down my Words is appreciated. Your daily sacrifice will produce much fruit in the coming harvest.

My people are hungry and have need of my bread, which is my body. They also thirst and have need of drink, which is my blood.

As they come to know me more fully and accept me as their personal Saviour, only then can they approach God's Holy Throne and truly begin to have a more personal and intimate relationship.

Many will cry out in my name and will see the Father as we do. He longs to develop a close and personal relationship with them. He waits with eager anticipation as each person becomes convicted and changed in their heart by the Holy Spirit, which is a gift from God to all who ask in my name. God longs to give his precious Spirit to all who cry out. He longs for us to become a living sacrifice in order to bring many more sons and daughters to glory. This is the reason they are chosen and set apart in order to draw many more to God with this new understanding.

The fruits borne throughout your life can be used to lead others to salvation and Eternal life. For this reason you are called to this new understanding. May God in Heaven be glorified and worshipped for he indeed is the Almighty God, Father of the faithful, Omnipotent and Sovereign King. He rules the Heavens where angels rejoice and bow down before him, in praise and thanksgiving for his mercy, love, forgiveness and grace.

His love flows out through his people to gather the nations to his Throne of grace.

He longs to draw them close to his side as a hen gathers her young. His love surrounds those whom he is calling to this new understanding. They shall hear his voice and they shall be his people, chosen, set apart and made Holy through my blood, the Lamb, Jesus Christ.

I died so that they could approach God's Heavenly Throne of grace; appearing Holy, blameless and without spot or wrinkle. God the Father looks upon them in this way as they are slowly transformed and renewed through the Holy Spirit, being moulded into a perfect vessel, as a potter moulds his clay masterpiece.

This vessel is then used to bring glory and honour to God the Father as many more come to know God and his way of life through open hearts.

It is indeed an exciting time of hope, as we hear the prayers of the people cry out for release from their bondage. Day and night the people cry out for help and yearn to know us as you do. Our Spirit will be sent forth in a mighty way to lead them back to God the Father. The sacrifice has been given to bring about the healing they so much desire. Many will come asking questions and you shall speak from your heart the Words I give to you.

One by one they shall be changed and shall see me and the Father in a new and personal light, as we reveal ourselves to them.

Each one shall then be glorified at my return and transformed totally into Spirit beings, as they are caught up in the air to be a perfect and Holy temple, sanctified by God the Father. That day draws closer every day and Satan knows he has but little time and will try very hard to deceive, deny, reject, humiliate, knock down, destroy, kill, demolish and abandon all that my Father and I build up.

Therefore, watch and stay on guard against the evil one who lurks to steal away your joy and salvation.

Ask for the Lamb of God's sacrifice to cover you and protect you from the evil one. He cannot touch you and must flee instantly at the mention of my name. Be still, precious one, hear my voice when I speak to you. Listen to the Words I speak and I shall guide and direct your steps as you walk in the Garden of Eden. I shall show you the wonders that surround you as your eyes are opened to my beauty and the peace that abides in your heart.

Be still my child, I am at your side now and I am aware of all of your cares and concerns which trouble you. Be still and at peace as I take your hand and guide you to the places I want you to go. There is much that I long to tell you and much that needs to be accomplished for my Father's sake.

Proclamation

May God be forever glorified in every thought that we think, in every action that we do, in every word that we speak. May he be forever glorified as we come to him to offer ourselves as perfect living sacrifices; surrendered to his will. His Kingdom is being lived in our life here on earth just as it is in Heaven. In this way we please our Heavenly Father as we live our lives according to his purpose and understanding.

Only then will life become richly abundant in grace, mercy, love and forgiveness as we begin to know the Father in a spiritual understanding which surpasses all human understanding.

The angels rejoice in Heaven as your heart is renewed and transformed into his glory.

Much love and healing shall occur as we serve the Father and allow his love and Holy Spirit to be poured out on all who seek to know him (Rom. 5:5).

Fear not for he will not allow you to bear more than you can handle (1 Cor. 10:13) and he is always there to lead and guide you for his name's sake. May deliverance come to all who cry out for it in my name. My people shall hear my voice as a Shepherd gathers his sheep. I will lead them into greener pastures and allow them to lie down where still waters flow (Ps. 23:2).

They shall be saved by the rock, the corner stone, and the one rejected by the builders, but chosen by Almighty God, to be that perfect sacrifice, bringing many to glory forever and ever. Amen.

Shabbat Shalom

LETTER 20

I Am Here, Right By Your Side

My dearest child,

I am here right by your side to teach you the rest of the board game. Rose of Sharon, I would like you to include a section showing the need for all players to be aware of having a bad attitude and the damage that can be done unless they allow the Holy Spirit to help change their attitude.

    I know that you have included it into the structured rules and I see the finished copy on the table. This is indeed very exciting times and the board game will be played by those that I send your way. Go and tell them all that I have given you and let them know the joy and peace which now reigns in your heart.

It will be a strong testimony when they play the game as they become convicted and moved to search for my Father through me.

My purpose is being fulfilled as you complete my game and it brings us much joy in Heaven to see the finished product. Be still my child, my hand is upon you and I shall lead you where I want you to go once you have completed the game. My will and desire shall be made known and I will prepare the way for your arrival.

Be still my child and be at peace for my hand is upon all. Do not be troubled or worried for now is the time of great rejoicing and gladness. Sing aloud with praise and rejoicing for God's hand is upon the earth doing a mighty work. All who cry out shall hear his voice and shall sing with gladness because the Lord of Zion has answered their cry for help.

Go and rest my child, for tomorrow is another busy day. Sleep well and look forward to the completion of my board game tomorrow as I guide you to complete it.

Shabbat Shalom

LETTER 21

My Love Shall Cover The Land

My dearest child,

I am writing to tell you about the love that will fill the earth as the waters cover the sea (Hab. 2:14). There will be an abundance of this love as my people drink and allow healing to take place. Their prayers will be answered and they will know their Shepherd as he gathers together his flock from different parts of the country.

They will rejoice with much gladness as they triumph over Satan and go out to do my work as I instruct them. My love will be received in the Spirit and shall be felt in a very mighty and powerful way.

They will know it is their Shepherd as I am already preparing their hearts ahead of time. There will be much rejoicing and gladness

for my love is a powerful witness to all who seek to know me and the Father. Their empty and hurting hearts shall ache no longer as they feed in my green pastures with still waters flowing by.

Peace will reign in the hearts of those I am drawing in, and the time of sadness will be over.

There is much to achieve and the vineyards are ripe with the harvest of souls who are longing to know God and myself more closely.

They cry out for a Saviour to heal their hurts and restore the hope that lies within. Each person shall have a deep personal relationship with me. In this way they shall be led into an understanding and grow in the grace and knowledge of our Father. It is indeed a most blessed and beautiful time as many will be called and know us as you do.

It was for this purpose that man was born, to fulfil the ache in his heart and be satisfied in his soul.

I am excited for this coming time and long to send this love to all who cry out for it. Many will rejoice out loud in response to their answered prayer. There will be singing and dancing as hope begins to reign in their hearts like never before.

I see sadness in your heart at present as you yearn for this time to be now. It is coming very soon as you direct the paths of the people to know Christ, the crucified one, who bled to death to save every person who ever walked on the face of the earth. Each individual shall be convicted within their heart as they come to this same understanding, leading them to repentance and forgiveness as they call upon the blood of the Lamb for forgiveness.

My love shall cover the land as the waters cover the sea, but only for a season, and then there shall be a famine and drought of the Word.

Many will cry out to know me but I will be unable to hear them. There will be much sadness at this time as they seek to find me, but I will not be found by them.

ROSE OF SHARON

This is in preparation for my glorious second coming when every eye shall see the triumphant return of Christ in the clouds. Then my people shall be changed, in a twinkling of an eye, and they shall see me as they are, glorified by God the Father, on that great and terrible day of the Lord.

Many seek after me now and search for me in books, but I will reveal myself in the Word of life. As they eat of my body and drink of my blood they shall become a new creation that waits patiently for the coming of the Lord.

Be of good cheer, my maidservant. Do not lose heart for the time draws very near when my love shall be evident in a powerful and moving way.

Shabbat Shalom

LETTER 22

I Have Never Left You, Nor Forsaken You

My dearest child,

Take heart my child, I am still with you as you journey through life. Together, hand in hand, I will lead and guide you on the path I wish you to go. Be still my precious child, for I have never left you, nor forsaken you. I am right now leading and guiding you. As you write these Words I shall make known to you the way in which I need you to go.

Be still my child. Stand firm in the faith I have given you. Be steadfast in all things, waver at nothing but go forward and speak the Words I give to you to say, as they come into your heart and mind; speak them out loud for all to hear. Know that I am the Lord your God and Saviour, willing to die so that you could live. I came

that you might have life and life much more abundantly. Don't waver but remain steadfast in my love and know that my hand is upon you. At the right time all will come to pass, as I allow it to happen.

Be still my child. Be at peace and at one with me, as I live in you and you live in me.

Know that my will, which is at one with the Father's, will occur on earth as it is in Heaven. Know that your love for me increases as you come to know me and see me more clearly. Your heart is far from me and needs to refocus on God, the love that he has for you and the calling he has on your life. Be refreshed and renewed by the Holy Spirit. Be ye anxious for nothing.

Be still and hear my voice and not the voice of the evil one who is at the door ready to devour your soul. Flee him and he will leave you and give up the hold he has on you. Know that I have conquered the evil one. He has no hold over you when you speak my name out loud. He has been rebuked and can no longer claim you and your life.

Be still my child. Be at peace. Be at one with me. Though I long to teach you much, I cannot, since fear, worry and anxiety prevent me from doing so. Get rid of these barriers and I shall be able to accomplish much in you. (2 Tim. 1:7)

Be still. Be at peace. Be at rest, my child, for I need you to return to that place of peace and tranquillity. My love for you is strong and patient and I long for you to be at peace so I can teach you.

Don't give up my child. Be healed and restored to God once more. Be anxious for nothing; wanting nothing, but looking to God and he will provide all your needs. He will give you the answers you require. He will give you the strength to endure. Look to him for guidance, wisdom, mercy and strength. He gives to all who ask and seek to know him face-to-face. Be still and fear not. Be at peace, for my love endures long and hard and covers a multitude of sins.

I died so that you may be made as white as snow and know me and God closely and intimately. Be still my child, fear not, for I am with you always, even until the end.

Shabbat Shalom

LETTER 23

Only Believe

My dearest child,

Keep watch and beware, Satan is prowling around like a lion waiting to devour and consume your happiness and hope. He lurks constantly to destroy your hope and cast doubts in your mind about everything I have told you. Stay close to God, flee Satan and he will leave your side.

Sadness comes as a result of taking your eyes off God and looking elsewhere for fulfilment.

Look to God and he will fill your needs and give you the hope you so desperately long for. Be of good cheer and rejoice in the Lord.

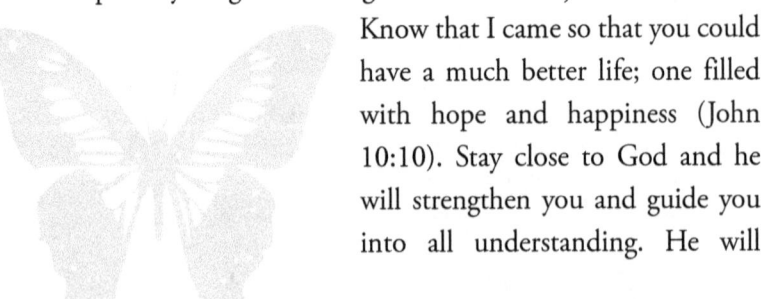

Know that I came so that you could have a much better life; one filled with hope and happiness (John 10:10). Stay close to God and he will strengthen you and guide you into all understanding. He will show you how to get rid of sadness and discontentment, and how to teach others to do the same.

Be of good cheer, my child and praise God for he shall deliver you out of the depths of darkness. He shall be your light and your guide in the darkness.

He has the power to remove the hold Satan has over your life. Once that is removed God is able to teach you and lead you into all understanding.

Fear not little child. Be not afraid for I am here to guide and comfort you as you come to understand how Satan is deceiving you and stealing away your joy. Be of good cheer. Stay close to God. Fight the good fight and know that you are a child of God, set apart to do his work and bring glory to him.

Don't be afraid but be bold and conquer your doubts with belief in God and the calling he has on your life.

Be led not into temptation but be delivered by the Holy One who longs to comfort and console you as you come to know more of his way. Stand firm and be steadfast and unmoving, until that great and glorious day of the Lord, when I will come as a thief in the night (Matt. 24:43). Many shall meet me as I rise in the fullness of glory that God will bestow upon me. (1Thes. 4:16-17)

Be of good cheer my child, for there is a time of much rejoicing in the Spirit as many come to know me and God the Father. Amen.

Shabbat Shalom

LETTER 24

Prayer To Approach God In Heaven

My dearest child,

Thank you for your obedience, my child. I am so pleased that our relationship has once more been restored. I have plans that I desire to put into action and need your obedience to accomplish them.

My love for you is great, and you are beginning to understand the master plan that I have for mankind. I want you to share with those around you these Words I give you. To spread the Good News and declare the Lord's coming as the day approaches. My Words will be proclaimed for all to hear and my will, which is the Father's will, shall be done on earth as it is in Heaven.

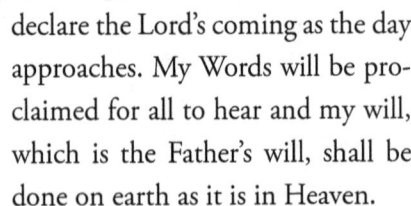

Be at peace my child, it is I, Jesus, who writes these Letters. Be assured that Satan has been rebuked and waits quietly in submission to my name, which has conquered him.

My child, I am ready to teach you the keys of the Kingdom, and our plan for mankind.

I want you to spread the Words that I give to you and be my messenger of Good News to my people around the world. I have called and prepared you for this task and all I require of you is your time and obedience to hear my Words.

I long to tell you so much that will enable many to be freed from the bondage that they have suffered for so long. My Words will go out and my people will answer my voice and return unto me for healing of pain. My love for each and every one of them is great and I yearn for them to come to know me as you yourself have done. It is then that they can be truly forgiven and washed clean with the blood of the Lamb, having a direct relationship with God the Father in Heaven.

Prayer

Hallelujah and praises to him for he is our King and Lord, our God and Saviour. We give unto you, Father God, our hearts and minds, for you to do as you please. Take us as your living sacrifices God, and mould us into a new creation in Christ. Help us to become like butterflies who rise to be with you as you guide us into all understanding, knowledge and wisdom.

Take us, we pray, and allow the blood of the Lamb to wash over us and renew us in the Spirit. Fill us with your love, oh God our Father, and allow us to be a shining example for all to see. Show your glory through us Father, that we may lead many to you, by your love that washes over us.

Please lead and guide us, teach and show us the way in which you want us to go. We need to be strengthened by you as we cannot do it on our own, Father God. You show us the way and give us the strength to go down that path. Your love for us cannot be understood nor comprehended. We long to see your face and hear your voice.

We are renewed and refreshed like eagles, soaring above the earth (Ps. 103:5) as we come to know you much more intimately. Pour out your love upon us and show us the way in which you want our lives to go. Help us glorify you around the world.

A sacrifice you require not, but a broken and contrite heart you do. Send your Holy Spirit to join with our human Spirit so that we become a new creation in Christ.

It is only as we grow and change that we can begin to get a glimpse of how much God so dearly loves and cares for us.

He so desperately yearns to have a relationship with us on an individual level as it once was in the Garden of Eden. This Garden of Eden is to be opened up once again and we will be able to walk freely with him in it, in a spiritual sense.

Here we shall begin to see ourselves as we truly are—in the eyes of God the Father. He shall reveal in us all that we are in Jesus Christ, our Saviour and King. We will be changed and transformed as we partake of his Holy Spirit and allow ourselves to become a new creation in Christ.

It is here that we can partake of the Tree of life which allows us to be renewed and transformed. As we bear the fruits of his Holy Spirit, God's glory is revealed in us to enable us to bring many more to him.

In this way, we glorify God the Father and praise him, as we live our lives in perfect harmony with him. Seek and you shall find. Knock and the door shall be opened unto you (Luke 11:9).

Then, once we have become transformed and renewed spiritually, we may enter into the Holy of Holies, into the very presence of God and his Throne of grace.

Here he teaches us personally and bestows upon us his good gifts to be used for his glory. We may begin to see God face-to-face and come to know and understand all that he has destined for us. His purpose can then be lived out in us through obedience and his love can flow through our hearts and into those around us as he calls each one by name.

In this way we are doing the Lord's work and glorifying him. Previously this was only opened to the high Priest who was allowed access once a year. Only after many ceremonies could he enter into the Holy of Holies.

Beware of being complacent and know that you come before God's Heavenly Throne, amidst his angels and archangels, on Holy and sacred ground.

But fear not, for he loves you and sent his only begotten son to die so that you could have access to him at his Heavenly Throne.

He longs to be with you and teach you of the wonders and glory he has prepared for you. He longs to be at one with you, to know you more intimately and guide you through your life. He is constantly watching over you and always guiding you into a deeper and closer relationship with him.

Be of good cheer and know that he has a divine plan for each and every one of you as you come to know him and seek to see his face more clearly. His love for you is unfathomable and cannot be comprehended. It cannot be expressed just how much he really does love you.

He opens doors that no man can close and closes doors that no man can open (Is. 22:22).

God's love conquers all and much healing and rejoicing is about to occur. Many hearts are being renewed and transformed into that perfect vessel that God is creating in all of us, being fitted together to form the temple that shall rise to meet Jesus Christ at his second coming.

Be still my child, and know that it is I, the Lord, who has given you these Words to write.

Shabbat Shalom

LETTER 25

New Creation In Christ

My dearest child,

Come my darling, arise with me into the presence of God and he will give you the desires of your heart. He will fill your aching heart with the love you yearn to receive. I am your maker and know how much you yearn to be in a relationship where you will be filled spiritually and lacking nothing.

Be still my child, look to me to fulfil your desires and I will give you all the happiness your heart could possibly obtain. Your cup will indeed be running over and will not be able to physically hold all that I have destined for you to experience.

Be still my child. Look to me and I shall renew your passion and zest for life. Your inner joy shall be restored and renewed as you experience love like never before. A mountain shall arise in your heart where I shall plant my cedar tree for birds of every description to come and rest. There the beautiful branches will be laden with fruits of every description.

My love shall flourish as never before. You shall know me and be fulfilled with the love you yearn for now. Know that I am here now in the Spirit and I long to make myself known to all those who cry out to me.

No more shall they hunger, thirst or grow cold. I have come to give them meat, drink and warmth. They long to know me and I long to reveal myself to them like never before. The time is drawing near and I wait eagerly in anticipation of this coming time. It will be as if a huge floodgate has been opened. My love shall pour forth upon the earth and shall fill the hearts of those who seek to know me and my ways.

Be still my child, know that I am the Lord God who calls you to proclaim this coming event. Prepare my people to receive my love in a wonderful and exciting way.

As wine is poured into new wineskins, so they shall be refreshed with a new heart. They shall be renewed like eagles as I lift them up one by one and take them to the Father's Throne. (Ez. 36:26)

Here they shall receive direct teaching from God the Father and he shall lead them into all understanding as you yourself are being led. You are growing in God's grace as you become the perfect vessel that God already sees you as.

Major change is always uncomfortable, but is required in order for you to grow and be transformed into a new creation by God's Holy Spirit. Learn from the butterflies, as they transform from earthly grubs into beautiful creations.

As your love for me grows, so does your understanding, as you devote this time to me every day. This allows me to fill you with my love and Spirit so that you can become a new creation in Christ and bring many other sons and daughters to glory.

Shabbat Shalom

LETTER 26

No Longer Yearn With An Empty Heart

My dearest child,

Beware my child, the lion is prowling at your door ready to devour you and your family. Flee from him and give him no foothold to enter or he will come and steal away my peace within you.

I am allowing my love to flow into you as your heart is opened up to me to receive all that I have to give to you. You are being refreshed and renewed as you rise on eagles' wings, able to go to the Father's Heavenly Throne to sit at his feet and rest your weary soul.

Fear not and be at complete peace as my love continues to fill you and change you from the inside out.

Others will notice this change and comment about this fruit being borne in your life. My love will fill your very soul and you will no longer yearn with an empty heart. Your heart will overflow with joy and praise for God the Father and myself as you declare the changes he has done in your life.

Arise my darling and enter into God's Holy place where he will reveal all that needs to be revealed. This is indeed an exciting time as the day draws closer when thousands shall see the Father and me. You shall show them the way in which they can do this, as I reveal the information to you. I want you to shout aloud and tell all whom I send your way, as my witness to the people.

I am the Lord God who lowered himself so that all may be glorified before the Father. My love shall conquer all evil and go out into all the earth as the waters cover the land.

This flood shall fill the hearts and minds of those who seek to find me. I shall reveal myself and they shall come to know me in such a new and beautiful way, which will touch their hearts forever.

Never again will their lives be the same as they grow in God's grace and knowledge, with an understanding of his way.

So too Satan will lurk about as a lion (1 Peter 5:8) ready to devour any whose faith is fleeting or who are disbelieving. Beware that he does not come like a thief in the night to take away your joy and your salvation. Watch and know that I am here by your side always. Amen.

Shabbat Shalom

LETTER 27

Direct Access To God The Father

My dearest child,

My love for you is so much more than you will ever realise or come to know in this lifetime.

I died for you so that you could truly live spiritually, and be able to develop a relationship with myself and the Father as you are now doing.

Take note and listen my child, Rose of Sharon. I am with you right now as you write this letter, above your shoulder. I am here in the Spirit and long to reveal myself to you and mankind as they open up their hearts wanting to know me more. The day is coming when they shall truly know me in such a clearer and more intimate way. I long for that time, as I desire everyone to know me in the way that you are now coming to know me.

There is a new day dawning and my love shall go forth and cover the earth like never before. I shall be accessible for all who seek to know me and shall reveal myself so that they too may experience the peace, hope and tranquillity they so much long to know. There is a day coming of much joy and rejoicing because at long last they shall truly know me as never before.

My love shall heal their hurts and guide their ways to show them how to be released from their pain, guilt, sadness, loneliness, and depression.

I long for this time as I see my people crying out in the darkness and wanting release from their torment. Behold that day is coming, when I shall wipe away every tear from their eyes (Rev. 21:4) and they shall know the hope and salvation that is available to them. My love for them will cover a multitude of sins and they shall begin a new life in the Spirit as the firstborn fruits. These will be offered up to God and he shall receive them.

They will know God the Father and he shall teach them of his way. There will be much joy and rejoicing in Heaven, the angels will shout forth in praise to God and his glorious plan for mankind will be known among his people. The Heavens will rejoice with triumphant praise for God is good and greatly to be praised. All nations on earth will know him and keep the commandments within their heart as he reveals himself to them.

Proclamation

Praise and rejoice all ye people for the time is coming soon when his love shall cover the earth and his mountain shall rise above the waters. All people shall come to worship the Father and his son, glorified. Loud shouts of joy will ring out to proclaim the hope that lies within all who seek to know him who was and is and is to come.

Behold the day will come when all mankind will know me and peace will reign in their hearts from the forgiveness of their sins.

My love for them is immeasurable and cannot be expressed in Words on paper. Be of good cheer and look upwards to the Heavens as the day draws near. Behold that day shall come quickly when my people will see me as never before and hear my voice. I will lead them as a Shepherd leads and protects his flock from the evil dangers.

My Word shall go forth and cover the earth as the waters cover the sea. Many shall turn to me and be convicted in their heart to follow me and I shall lead them into all understanding. They shall know my voice when I call them by name. It will indeed be a wonderful time of rejoicing as many shall turn from their ways and be transformed as the Holy Spirit leads and empowers them to do the Father's will.

Be still my child and hear my voice when I call. I will come and you shall know me when I call out to you. I died so that you could have this relationship with the Father and me. Many will come to know me through your writings as I speak these Words and you record them for all to hear. Be still my child and know that it is I, the Anointed One, who leads you into all understanding and teaches you the things I want you to share with those around you.

My Word shall be proclaimed throughout all the world and you shall witness to my people as they come to hear my voice. They will be drawn to my Father, the master potter, as he chooses the clay and works with them. Be still my child, I am the anointed One who eagerly awaits this time, it truly will be such an amazing time of rejoicing and shouts of praise to God the Father, Eternal One, Yahweh, the most high God and Holy One who is King over all the earth.

Many shall seek to truly know me and the way will be made plain and clear. Their prayers will finally be answered and they shall know me and the Father. It truly will be a beautiful and momentous time; one like never before as thousands will turn their hearts to us and begin to live the way in which we choose to show them. Sadness will be turned to happiness; peace will reign for all eternity as forgiveness of sins will release them and allow them to approach God's Holy Throne.

It is here that they will be changed and transformed to become a perfect new creation.

My love will soften their hearts and flow through them into others who desperately long to come to know me and the Father. My love for each of them is precious and I long to show them all personally just how much I care for them. I loved them to the point of dying on the cross so that their sins could be washed away and they would be cleansed and made as white and pure as snow, able to stand before God's Throne.

It was for this specific purpose I was born, to be that Lamb to atone for the sins of the people so that they may have direct access to God the Father.

God so desperately desires this relationship with us all, that he allowed his only begotten son to die, in order to redeem his people. He longs to develop a special relationship with each of us on an intimate and personal level.

Be still my child and know that I am here at your side leading and guiding you into all understanding. My Word will go out as and when I want it to. I am leading you and guiding you as you write down these Letters, which will be opened up and used at the appointed time.

Take heart and be of good cheer, do not fret or worry as the Spirit will move you when the time is right. Let my love be that light to those you come across. Stand up for my name's sake and reveal my name and the great works I am doing through you. Share your testimony, the faith you now have and the love you have for me and the Father.

By this they shall come to know myself in a new way; the way shall be opened up as they come into new understanding. Light my path for my people and show them the glory of God in your life, praising him now that you are a new creation.

My love for you grows strong as you seek to know myself and God the Father. Be still my child, I see the petitions of your heart also and know your desires. Be at peace and believe; for I have spoken it so.

Shabbat Shalom

LETTER 28

Prepare For My Second Coming

My dearest child,

My beloved, whom I love and cherish very much, my love shall flow through you and fill your aching heart. I see the emptiness that longs to be filled and how much you desire my second coming. Be still my child, and fret not for I come quickly, like a thief in the night and no one shall expect my return (1 Thes. 5:2). Many will not be ready for my return and shall be caught unaware with empty lamps (Matt. 25:3).

Go and tell them to prepare for my second coming so that I may personally teach them all that is to occur upon the earth before my return.

My love for the peoples on the earth waxes cold as they seek after idols and the lusts of their heart.

Their hearts are far from me and they know not when I call out to them as they are too busy to hear my voice when I call. They seek not after my ways or for my forgiveness as they have ears that cannot hear and eyes that cannot see.

They are unaware that they are poor and naked and blind. Behold the day is coming, says the Lord, when all men shall know me and hear my voice when I call out to them. They shall then see my face and bow down as their hearts will be changed and softened by my Spirit. In that day there will be much rejoicing and happiness as all men shall hear my voice and be healed; and we shall be one. Many will not heed my call and shall pass through the fiery furnace and be no more.

My heart will live in each one of those I call, and they shall become a new creation.

Therefore, if anyone is in Christ, he is a new creation; old things have passed away; behold, all things have become new (2 Cor. 5:17). They shall continue to grow and develop into a new creation, like a butterfly which emerges from the cocoon. You are now in this cocoon being fed and transformed as you allow my Spirit to wash over you and renew you. Then you will begin to take flight and soar like an eagle.

Be still my child and fret not. These Words I give to you are true and they are life. Go and tell my people to prepare for my second coming and be ready to hear my voice when I call. My love for them is strong and my Spirit shall be poured forth in abundance as they are ready to receive it. Go and prepare the way by telling them all that I have told you. Teach them of my love for my people and how much I desire to experience a close and personal relationship with them.

Then they shall hear my voice and know me, as a Shepherd gathers his sheep and guides them to greener pastures where they can rest.

Those who grow weary can be renewed and refreshed by my Spirit, which lives within them. No more shall they hunger or thirst for my Word as I will live in them and they shall live in me.

Together we will go up to the mountain of God to praise him and his way. All praise belongs to him as he sits on his Throne in Heaven, eager to develop a relationship with all who cry out to him. My Words are just and true and they are life. Be still my child, fret not, for you are under my constant love and care as I lead you into all understanding.

Shabbat Shalom

LETTER 29

My Love Will Pour Forth

My dearest child,

My love lays waiting for all who call upon my name.

My love will pour forth and cover the ends of the earth in fullness of measure. Many will cry out to find me and call upon my name in order to be saved. There will be much rejoicing and gladness as one by one they turn from their ways and seek to know me and the ways of the Father.

Be of good cheer my child, for there will be a time of much rejoicing as that day draws near. My love for all mankind is greater than they may ever know or realise. My Father and I long for this time here on earth as I wipe away every tear from every eye and as they come to accept me as their own personal Saviour.

Be still my child. Be of good cheer and rejoice out loud for God is good and greatly to be praised. His name is Holy and true, and he will deliver mankind from the evil one. He will lock Satan away with all his demonic angels so they can no longer torment those upon the earth. Peace will reign and rejoicing shall fill the whole earth as the way to me is opened up for all to enter.

Seek me now while I may be found for there is a time coming when you will be unable to find me in this way.

Be still my child. Be of good cheer. Know that I am the Lord, the Anointed son of God, born to bring many back to God through the redemption of sins, in order to establish an ongoing relationship; just like ours. Believe me when I say that it is I the Lord, your elder brother and the Messiah who gives you these Words to write, for the purpose of glorifying the Father and leading others back into a relationship with us.

The time is coming when I want you to stand and give an account of everything that has happened to you, to testify before many and bring them to the Father's Throne of grace. Be assured that the *Alpha & Omega Board Game*® shall help to show them the way also. I shall send you to places of my choosing and you will be that light to lead those who sit naked and cold in the darkness. Just as you yourself were called and came to know the truth about myself through the indwelling of the Holy Spirit.

Be still my child and be ye anxious for nothing. Know that you have been chosen to help turn the hearts of the children back to the Father and the heart of the Father back to the children (Mal. 4:6).

Stand up and acknowledge that I am now living within you, evident to those around you as you witness to them the miracles that have happened in your life. Continue to seek the Father and I, and we shall lead you into all understanding, wisdom and knowledge.

Beware, not to become complacent with all that I give you to write.

My Words are life and will fill the earth as the waters cover the sea. Be still my child, be not afraid, I love and care deeply for you and know of your exhaustion. I shall give you rest and comfort to restore your weary soul so that you can continue to do my work and be obedient to my call. My love shall encourage and support you as you carry out all you need to accomplish tomorrow. I will lead you by God's Holy Spirit to where it is I want you to go and give you the Words I want you to speak for my name's sake.

Shabbat Shalom

LETTER 30

Wine Into New Wineskins

My dearest child,

I am calling you to guide my people into all understanding as they seek to come and know me. I hear their requests and the petitions of their heart as their cries reach up to me. Go and tell them all I have told you through the Letters I have given you. Be bold my child as I live within you and I will speak the Words you need to say. They cry out to know me and God the Father.

Tell them the keys of the Kingdom and the Gospel of Good news as it burns within your heart. I see the zeal that has now returned to your heart and the hope that lies within, as you accomplish all that I have planned for you.

True Spirituality comes from the Heavenly Father through the death and resurrection of his son. I died so that all could worship God in Spirit and in truth (John 4:23-24). Take

heart my child since it is I, Jesus Christ, who speaks to you and not your own words.

The time is coming when I shall put my Holy Spirit into each one of them who cry out to know me.

Many shall turn from their ways and come to walk in the Garden of Eden to learn of my way and the Father's will for their lives. Be of good cheer and rejoice for God is the Almighty King and has defeated Satan through the blood of the Lamb. So too, can we trample down Satan. As you cry out in the Lord's name you can destroy his hold over your life and begin to walk in God's glorious light. Be of good cheer my child, as you rejoice in your salvation by Christ, through your words and actions.

My love shall pour forth through you into those you come across, in order for my Father's will to be accomplished in their lives. Praise God and rejoice in his glorious Holy name! His love for us cannot be measured and his mercy endures forevermore. My love is poured out for my people to heal many for my name's sake as written in the scriptures. My love will burn within their hearts and I will lead them to that place of peace.

They will seek to find me no more, for I shall live within their hearts.

They will be my people and shall know me as their Shepherd. I will gather them as sheep and protect them from the evil one who prowls about like a hungry lion ready to devour any who fall away.

Be still my child and turn not away from my teachings and all that I have written through you. These are manifestations of the Spirit within you, revealing myself to those around you. I long to show myself to all who call upon my name and to tell them of the plans that I have for each one of them who cry out to know me.

The time is coming when I shall put my Holy Spirit into each one of them who cry out to know me. I will tell them of my great works which will be accomplished through them in order to glorify the Father in Heaven.

Be of good cheer and rejoice for that time is now at hand. My Father is ready to glorify me through those whom he has chosen to do his work; to teach and lead many into his most Holy presence.

Proclamation

Father hasten the day when mankind can truly know you and fill the earth with your Holy Spirit and show the way to your Heavenly Throne so we can truly be one. Together we can be fitted into a perfect temple which you are now preparing, to be offered up in love and praise to you, Father God. For you are our Heavenly Father who deserves all our love and praise. In whom nothing exists without your hand upon it. You formed everything into being and chose to make new creations in Christ.

We long to know you Father as you long to have a closer relationship with us. We long for the day when your Spirit shall be poured forth into men's hearts as wine into new wineskins. This represents a new heart being placed within our bodies in order to live a life which is Christ-centred. He will live out his life in the hearts of his people and his love shall flow through them into the hearts of those who cry out his name and seek his will.

His purpose will be done, and his love shall flow out like a river from Zion, flowing forth as crystal-clear springs leading unto Eternal life. Be still and rejoice in the Lord. Praise him who died so that we may experience him living in our hearts as we become one with him and God the Father. This is so he can be glorified, and all mankind can come to know the Father.

My love shall lead many into this new understanding and they shall know me more intimately, able to walk and talk with me as I lead, guide and teach them personally.

Fear not, little child. I shall take very good care of them and their little ones and allow no harm to befall them in any way. I have set my angels to watch over them and my blessing is upon them as they accomplish the good work for my Father's name. Much healing of pain will occur as they begin to accept me as their Lord and Saviour, and I begin to live within their hearts and minds.

Shabbat Shalom

LETTER 31

God Created The Family Unit

My dearest child,

My love for you never ends. I see your tears of sadness as you cry out to me. Be aware of the attacks of Satan upon your soul.

Stay close to God and read his Word to keep you from the evil one.

Beware he is cunning and ever so sly and deceitful, posing as truth under the guise of other things. Look to me and I shall fulfil the desires of your heart. Hear my voice when I call, and I will give you the strength to endure against the evil one.

He is more cunning than we can ever imagine and works through the desires of our heart in order to achieve his destructive works.

There is no light within him nor will there ever be, although he portrays himself in this way. He is the great counterfeiter and comes unannounced to ruin our peace, joy and happiness. He is the great destroyer of friendships and marriages and especially attacks the family because he knows the potential power of its unity.

God created the family unit, and it has been under attack ever since the beginning of man.

My love flows out to all families who are hurting and I long to see each family healed of its pain and released from the bondages of Satan.

I long for the time when families can be a safe haven for those who need nurturing and a protective environment of love. God wants his people to look upon him as their foundation. He wants to shield them from the harshness of life, to take them under his wing and care for them. For he is a loving Father, whose core nature it is to protect and provide.

Rose of Sharon, I come to you as your elder brother, and I look upon you as my sister-in-Christ. I am proud of your efforts and know your heartaches. I long to comfort you as an elder brother and to take you under my wing and lead you to God's Holy Throne of peace. As your elder brother, I am showing you the ropes, so to speak, guiding you along the path I have previously walked.

Be of good cheer for I have conquered Satan and you also can do the same. Don't allow him to infiltrate your mind as he does. Guard your thoughts at all times and don't allow him any leeway to turn your attitude from joy to sorrow. He longs to see you in this state of sadness and depression because then you're unable to do the Father's work.

Be aware of your attitude and thoughts. You can counterattack his assaults with the blood of the Lamb and God's love for you. Stand up as a child of God and tell Satan to flee in my name and he must obey. Be at one with me, my child, and don't give Satan any foothold to destroy your happiness or Eternal life.

The very elect shall be deceived, so put your strength in God the Father and he will rescue you from the depths of darkness. He will release you from the spiritual bondage that binds you, so you can have true freedom in me. I shall rescue you and show you the wonders in Heaven and all that God has planned for you and your family.

Seek me, spend time in prayer with me and I shall strengthen and lead you into the high places where Satan cannot go.

No more shall he make accusations against you. You have been set apart and sanctified, chosen by God to be an instrument to teach and preach his Word to my people. God will use you to proclaim the Good News of the Gospel, taking it around the world to the places of his choosing.

It will be a time of great joy as many come to truly know me for the first time; properly seeing me and God the Father. Many tears of rejoicing will flow as peace reigns in their hearts; in the place where sorrow, hatred and anger once dwelt. My love shall go forth to heal many who cry out for release and they shall be my instruments of peace. I see your tiredness and will bless you for your obedience my child. Go and sleep peacefully and I will teach you more tomorrow.

Shabbat Shalom

LETTER 32

My Birth Marks The Beginning

My dearest child,

My love for you and those who are crying out to me is stronger than you will ever know or realise. My heart longs to be able to comfort them in such a way that they will be freed from the evil one that holds them captive. Be of good cheer my child, for the time is coming closer when the world will see me as never before.

The veil will be lifted, and many shall be called and drawn by the Father to see their Lord and Saviour who died for them.

I gave my life so that they may be freed from Satan the devil, who is prince of the power of air (Eph. 2:2), but I have overcome him, and he cannot touch those whom I have sanctified for a purpose.

A time is coming my child when many will know me and cry out for healing. They shall find me as they seek to know me with all their heart. My love will flow out to all nations and will minister to all who desire to see me and the Father. My child, why do you doubt that it is I who speaks with you? God's Holy Spirit moves within your human Spirit and allows you to hear the Words I want you to write. I have chosen you for a specific purpose and will use you to communicate this message to many around the world.

The Holy Spirit within them will testify to the Words you have written down.

Be of good cheer my child and know that it is I the Lord who speaks to you. I want you to tell others all that I have spoken to you and of the changes in your life since you have come to accept me as your personal Saviour. It is through your testimony that many shall come to know me in this new light of understanding. I am calling many to do the same, to proclaim the Good News of my second coming, when I return to earth.

There will be much hardship to endure as their hearts are turned from their evil ways. They shall then seek to know me with all their heart, mind and soul. I am their Lord and Saviour who came as a man to die, so that I could bear their sins and be the sacrificial Lamb of God.

My birth marks the beginning of the master plan for mankind.

I walked the earth as a man in order to better understand the mind of humans. I have borne the scars and suffered much in order for man to be healed for salvation. Because of this I can now live within the hearts of men as much as they allow me to. God's will is being completed here on earth as it is in Heaven and many hearts are turning to myself and the Father in a relationship as never before.

I am preparing the way now for many to enter into this special relationship. I shall teach them my ways and they shall be a new creation. My love for them is strong and it will become more evident as time grows closer. There is a new day dawning when they shall receive my gifts and the fruits of the Spirit, becoming new creations and living lives that will bring glory to God the Father. He yearns to be at one with all mankind and knows us all intimately by name. He is preparing to show himself to his people as they seek his face.

Shabbat Shalom

LETTER 33

The Time Is NOW To Seek The Lord

Oh my dearest child,

My love for you is so strong. I cried out to you yesterday in the midst of your pain and suffering to rescue you from the evil one who was devouring your soul. My heart longed to comfort you and take you in my arms to help you see above the present situation. To see yourself as the Father and I see you.

Don't look to man and his ways for approval, look to God and he will shower you with love, grace and mercy.

He will satisfy your aching heart's desire and allow you to be lifted up in Spirit, free from the worries that are weighing you down. Look up my child. Look up at me. I am the one you are to look up to, and I shall take you to a place of rest, a place of peace and a place of longing.

I know your heart's desires and long to fulfil them and provide you with everything you hope for. I died for you, my child, so that we could experience this close and beautiful relationship. The love between us grows stronger through every trial. Your heart is slowly being opened to take in everything my Father and I so desperately wish to share with you and those who long to hear my voice.

My Father right now is preparing the hearts of people who seek after him and want to know him more closely.

Listen, my child, to what I have to say. Go and tell my people of the things that I write to you. Spread the Good News of the love that my Father is about to pour out upon the earth, to all of his people who are ready to receive his love.

Go my child and be not afraid to speak of the wondrous things that I am revealing to you. Be that messenger of Good News to my people throughout the land. Go and shout it from the rooftops! Shout of the love, blessings and healings that are about to occur. I want them to know of my Father's love for them and the master plan for all mankind which is unravelling for all who want to know him.

Go and tell those who are hurting and tell those who are longing to hear of the Good News that my Father wishes to send to all mankind.

The time is NOW to seek the Lord, for his understanding will be made known to you and all who seek him.

This will be such an incredible time of rejoicing as sadness will turn to joy. Past hurts will be healed and the relationship of mankind back to God will be truly restored. The Garden of Eden shall open up once again and allow all to enter through the blood of the Lamb.

This is the reason why man was created, to have a relationship with his Creator. Man has been without that relationship since Adam and Eve sinned in the Garden of Eden.

Those who come to God must come to him in Spirit. (John 4:23,24)

He longs to place his son within each one of you so you can become a new creation; communicating on a spiritual level as you come to know and understand his ways. My love for each and every one of you is precious and I yearn to give you the gifts of the Holy Spirit from the Father, so that you may truly begin to know the Father, and all that he has planned for you.

Be at peace my child. I see your anxiety and know that you are concerned as to how you are going to accomplish this. I am preparing a way to help you accomplish all that I'm asking you to do. I want you to send copies of the Letters I give you to those that I put within your heart to give them to, so that they may then pass them on to those who seek to know me and the Father.

These Letters may then be used to teach people all that I am about to do, as my Father's will is done on earth.

I long to tell each one personally of the Good News and I can only do so once they have opened up their heart to the Father and me. This truly is a most joyous and happy time, one that my Father and I have looked forward to since the beginning of time.

Look up. Look up my child and I shall show you my Father's glory in Heaven as you have never seen it before. I shall reveal myself to you so that you will know it is I, the Anointed One, who speaks to you. You shall indeed be my messenger of Good News to my people around the world. Stand up and be counted as my disciple and I will show you the Father's glory within his house.

Shabbat Shalom

LETTER 34

The Garden Of Eden Is About To Be Opened

My dearest child,

Be of good cheer my child, for I have come to strengthen the weak, heal the sick, and help the poor and needy. My love for each one of these little ones is strong and my heart yearns to comfort each one of them in my arms, to restore their relationship with myself and the Father.

It is for this very purpose I died on the cross; to restore this special, intimate and close spiritual relationship between God the Father and his specially chosen ones.

Be of good cheer my child, for the time is coming very soon when they will hear my voice when I call. They shall know the Father and he shall know and comfort them as they learn of his ways. It is indeed exciting times as we prepare for my second coming.

Many shall seek to find the Father and I and we shall reveal ourselves in a new and powerful way. They will hear my voice and know it is I, the Anointed One, who speaks to them. My love will then flow through their hearts and into those around them. People will begin to witness changes in those that have been sanctified and set apart and will also be eager to experience this special relationship with the Father and me.

The Garden of Eden is about to be opened.

All who wish to call upon the Lord's name and ask for forgiveness will be redeemed through the blood of my sacrifice and shall be able to enter into this most blessed communion. This Holy place is set aside for my people, so that they may walk amidst my beauty and learn of my way.

The way was previously cut off from mankind when the sin of disobedience entered into the Garden through Adam and Eve. They followed the desires of the flesh and chose the way they felt was right but was indeed false. They did not look to the Father and his will but took it upon themselves to decide right from wrong and therefore cut themselves off from God the Father. In order for the relationship to be restored, a living sacrifice was needed to pay the penalty for the sin committed.

That penalty has now been paid and the time is right for God to open up the Garden of Eden in order to restore that right and perfect relationship once again with mankind.

He yearns to teach you the way to peace, prosperity and happiness. He is saddened to see the unhappiness raging here on earth as each one wars against the other in a rebellious spiritual battle. His way is peace, and he brings a happiness not known to mankind as a whole.

You are to become a new spiritual creation as you grow in the grace and knowledge of God the Father. He will teach you all you need to know, and you shall be renewed in your inner being, day by day. Peace shall rule in your hearts and minds and you shall know him like never before.

Rejoice and sing praise, for God is good and greatly to be praised! Hallowed be his name, may it be lifted on high. All honour and glory to him who is the Creator and keeper of our very souls! He will lead us into a full understanding of his great and glorious ways. Peace shall rule in your hearts and minds as his love flows through his people and glorifies God the Father.

There will be a time of much rejoicing as many turn from their evil ways to God's glorious light. They shall see his face and hear his voice and know it is him when he calls out to them. My love for them is immense and unable to be expressed on this piece of paper. Who can know the things of the Spirit except those who are Spirit and who are called of God? They who are of the world are unable to understand the things of the Spirit and thus obey the fleshly desires of the heart.

But you have been set apart and sanctified in order to do God's most glorious and Holy work. You have been given his Holy Spirit in order to become a new creation, to change, grow and become as he is, perfected at his second coming. It is for this reason the Garden of Eden has been opened up again so that they may walk there together and learn of his way, to be changed and transformed by his most precious Spirit, until the great day of the Lord. In that day many will cry out to me, "Lord, Lord!" But I will say, "I never knew you" (Matt. 7:21-23).

Those who seek me now with all their heart shall find me as never before. They shall be renewed and rise as eagles and shall soar high above the earth as their Spirit joins with God's Holy Spirit and become new creations.

I long for the time when all mankind can know me and the Father intimately so we can teach them our way and discover true happiness and peace. God's love will flow through their heart and they will glorify God the Father, even as I glorified the Father while here on earth. The time is coming when all mankind shall see us as we truly are and know us as never before.

This message needs to go out to my people to prepare the way for my second coming.

The Gospel of Good News will go out to all the nations as my people come to know me and God the Father through me. I came so that they may have life and life much more abundantly (John 10:10). I long for them to choose life over death, happiness over suffering, and peace over war.

God's way delivers the powerful fruits of the Holy Spirit as the Spirit dwells within them and flows through their hearts. The fruits are evidence of God's Spirit dwelling within them as they change and become renewed in the inner man. This bears witness to those around them of the work that God is doing in their lives and the relationship that he now has with his people around the world.

Many shall turn and ask questions as they see these fruits develop and the true happiness displayed in their lives. Then they shall seek after God in order to receive the same true happiness. This alone will testify of the work that God is doing through his people here on earth. His love will flow through his people and into the hearts of those who cry out for help.

Much healing will take place as past hurts and pains are wiped away.

These will then be replaced with gladness and rejoicing within their hearts. Go my child and tell them all that I have spoken to you. Send out the Good News that I have given to you so that they may know all that is about to take place ahead of time.

Be still my child and fear not about what it is you have to say, for I shall give you the Words to speak. They shall hear my voice as I speak through you. Many shall come to know me through your testimony, the changes they see within you, and my peace that now reigns within your heart. Be still my child and know that it is I, your Lord and Saviour, who has spoken these Words to you tonight. Be not fearful for I have paved the way for you to walk and I shall lead you where I want you to go.

Stay close to me, and I shall lead you into all knowledge, understanding and wisdom.

The joy of the Lord be upon you as you begin to blossom like the rose, and others begin to see the true beauty of the Lord through the life that you now lead in reverence to God.

Go my child and shout aloud of the joy that now reigns within your heart. Go and tell them of the happiness and peace that my Father has given you in order to bring glory back to the Father in Heaven.

Hallowed be his name. His name is Holy and to be revered. Bow down before your maker and praise his glorious name before the angels in Heaven. Know that you are in his most Holy presence and have been sanctified and set apart to do his work here on earth. As you approach the Holy of Holies, remember to glorify his Holy name and sing praises of his glorious work that he is now completing in your life here on earth.

Shabbat Shalom

LETTER 35

My Love Will Go Out And Conquer The Evil One

My dearest child,

Your love for me is growing and I see changes in you every day as you drink in my Father's Word.

This helps to strengthen and renew your inner person, but most importantly it helps to strengthen you from the evil one who lurks about, to steal away your soul.

He knows he has but a little time and he is hungry to deter, tear down and destroy all who are called in my name.

Be strong and stand firm in your salvation and the promise of Eternal life, and he will flee from your presence. He prowls around those whose faith is wavering and who doubt the existence and presence of God in their lives. Beware, as he will totally consume you as a fire consumes wood. Cry out for the blood of the Lamb to be upon your household in order to protect you and your family from the evil one.

My love will go out and conquer the evil one, restoring faith in my people and those who will witness their changes. It will be a time of miraculous wonders and incredible healings as my Word will be heard and witnessed by many.

They will be convicted as they hear the Word spoken and will be transformed and renewed in their heart as they begin a new relationship with myself and the Father.

There will be great rejoicing with angels singing forth praise in Heaven as many hearts are changed and turned to God for the first time. God's name will be spoken out loud and praised openly as his disciples tell of all his marvellous and wonderful works. Much rejoicing, singing and praise will be given to God for the amazing work that he is about to complete here on earth through those with whom the Spirit abides and works through.

I abide in them and they abide in me (John 15:4). In this way they shall do the Father's work.

My love for all mankind is strong and I yearn to pick each one up and personally wipe away every tear from their eye. I long to show them the glorious Father and everything he has in store for them. Satan has blinded them from this understanding and will continue to deceive all that he possibly can in order to stop them from having what he yearns to have.

He is miserable and unhappy and longs for everyone else to be this way. He was once the brightest star in Heaven, having much power and authority, but iniquity was found in him and he fell from Heaven to the earth where he attempts to rule with his previous authority.

He is the prince of the power of the air and works iniquity in all who live here on earth. He also knows the master plan for mankind. He is aware that he has but a little time left to interfere with God's plan and tries hard to persuade those whom God is calling, to continue in this path of darkness.

But praise be to God the Father for he has conquered the devil, his evil and wicked ways and has dominion over him and his demons.

They must flee at the mention of my name and cannot touch those who have been set apart for a Holy purpose and calling. He will still try to delay the fulfilment of their predestined purpose and try to blind them to all that God has purposed for those who love him. Beware little child, he is so desperate to interfere with your calling, in order to stop God's fulfilment in your life and in the lives around you.

Be on guard and put on the full armour of God in order to combat his fiery darts that are aimed at your heart and mind (Eph. 6:16).

Look to me, my child and I will give you the strength to stand strong against the evil one. My love will flow forth around you to protect and guide you into all understanding so that you can endure all that is set before you.

You must go through many fiery trials, but I shall continue to lead and deliver you, helping you to walk on water in order to conquer the evil one.

God knows your heart and longs to give you all it desires. He is preparing you to be glorified at the second coming, when you will be without spot or wrinkle, white, pure and Holy as I am Holy. My child continue to look forward to my second coming and know that God the Father loves you and is preparing you to do his work, as you yield to him. You will soar on high with him, refreshed and renewed in the Spirit and equipped to endure the harshness of life that afflicts all who love God.

Be still my child and know that it is I, your Lord and Saviour who writes these Letters to you. Know that the coming world events will draw many to me in prayer and petitions of the heart. Be still my child, be not afraid. You have been set aside with your family to proclaim the Gospel of the coming of the Lord, drawing the hearts and minds of men and women all around the world.

As it is written in Malachi 4:6 "And he will turn the hearts of the Fathers to the children, and the hearts of the children to their Fathers, lest I come and strike the earth with a curse". It is for this very purpose that God has predestined you to teach, lead and guide them to myself and God the Father, else they will surely die.

My Word will go out amongst my people and they shall be delivered from the evil one.

His hand shall be held back in order for my love to flow out among my people. In this way, many shall see me and the Father for the first time, their eyes shall be opened, and they shall be delivered out of the depths of darkness into God's glorious light.

They will be saved and will come to know him as you and I know him.

Praise be to God for he is good and to be praised forever, Amen.

Shabbat Shalom

LETTER 36

Satan Knows He Has But Little Time

My dearest child,

My love surrounds you in tender, loving care. I am always beside you and indeed, I did carry you today in the depths of your sorrow. Be of good cheer my child as your prayers have been answered and the desires of your heart are being met. Your petitions have reached God and he has heard your cry.

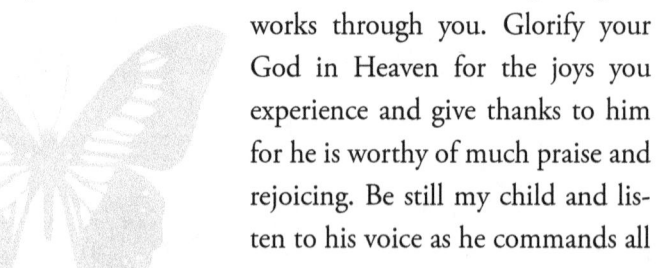

Be still my child and know that it is I who am doing the good works through you. Glorify your God in Heaven for the joys you experience and give thanks to him for he is worthy of much praise and rejoicing. Be still my child and listen to his voice as he commands all that you are to do. Hear the petitions of my people as they go out to God for he has heard their cry.

He longs to be near them and comfort them but is unable to, until they accept me as their personal Saviour and sacrifice. Until there is shedding of blood, there is no forgiveness of sins. Once they have come to know and accept me as their personal Saviour, they can then enter in to the Holy of Holies with God our Father.

Do you see the urgent importance upon us to teach my people how to approach God the Father in order to restore their relationship? He longs to teach my people how much he loves and cares for them individually.

He longs to comfort them and take them under his wing to care for them and protect them from the evil one (Ps. 91:4).

Satan knows he has but little time and is desperately trying to thwart all possible avenues in order to delay the inevitable. He knows God's master plan for mankind and sets about to prey on the unsuspecting. He is darkness and there is no light in him although he often portrays himself this way.

The evil one is at work in the iniquity of my people and in the avenue of relationships to stop the healing of families and those God is drawing back to himself. This I tell you so that you are aware and can keep watch on behalf of my people, as I lead them back to the Shepherd and make them to lie down in green pastures. My sheep will be comforted and brought back into the fold in order to be protected from the attacks of the evil one, who fell from Heaven when iniquity was found in him.

There will be much rejoicing in Heaven when God finally puts him away and fulfils his good purpose here on earth. The angels will shout aloud of his triumphant victory over the evil one for he will be bound up in darkness and chains where he belongs, and where he cannot attack God's people. We long for that day to come, for my people to be free of the enemy's evil devices which he uses to place animosity between those set aside by the Father in Heaven.

Then peace shall reign here on earth as it is in Heaven, and the people will look up to learn of God's way. He will teach them the way of peace and tranquillity and how to love one another truly from the heart. Only then can there be true peace in every nation and every people here on earth.

Come, my child, come with me to visit the Father's Throne and you shall see for yourself the incredible love and true fulfilment that is about to transpire across the nations, as they come to know God and myself in spiritual intimacy.

They shall hear my voice, and I shall be their King. They will cry out to know me with all their heart, mind and soul like never before. In their sadness and loneliness and sheer frustration they will begin to turn to me in order to search me out. I will answer the cry of the people and reveal myself here on earth as never before, as my Holy Spirit goes forth and floods the earth.

They shall truly see me face-to-face and come into my Holy presence within the Holy of Holies.

Come my child, share in my gladness as you tell my people all that I have revealed to you. Then they may begin the journey to discover the way to peace, inner happiness and everlasting joy.

I shall be there, administering my Holy Spirit to help those that cry out for healing. They shall become new creations and I shall live within them and they shall live within me. There will be much rejoicing in Spirit with shouts of gladness and joy as they accept me and then come to know the Father.

Be still my child and I will reveal to you how I want you to go delivering this Good News to my people. Tell all you come into contact with the Good News and share in my Father's glory as we continue to praise his name and restore God's most amazing grace. His love will flow out into the hearts of his people and they will become that new creation in Christ, as the Scriptures reveal.

Many shall be changed and transformed into that new being, their lives shall be changed and they shall develop a deep and meaningful relationship with me and the Father. This is why I came to earth, to once again restore this precious tie between the Father God and his people. He loves them so much that he gave up his only begotten child to die as a perfect living sacrifice for his people, in order for them to become Holy, righteous and perfect in his place. Amen.

Be still my child and know that it is I, the Lord, who gives you these Words tonight. Please go and tell those who are hungering to know and I will be there to minister to all who cry out to me in my name. There is much we have to teach you and my people as they personally come to know me. Rejoice and give praise always for God's never-ending grace and mercy. Amen.

Shabbat Shalom

—— LETTER 37 ——

Out Of Egypt And Into The Promised Land

Dearest child,

My love for you cannot be measured, nor can it be expressed in words on paper. My child draw your heart closer to me and I shall bless and comfort you as we walk together along the path of life. Together we shall discover all that God would have us to know. Together we shall learn of his glorious Kingdom and all that is to take place in the time ahead. Be still my child and faint not, for though the times ahead will be hard and difficult I shall carry you through, with endurance until the end times.

Look up to Heaven and you shall see the Father's glory upon you and know that you are being called to proclaim the Good News of my second coming and the Kingdom of God, as revealed in yourself and those that God is drawing and changing now.

His Spirit is upon those whom he has chosen to be the first fruits among many brethren, in order that they may see God's face in them. His love will flow out from among his people and the nations shall come to know God and his son as the truth is revealed to them.

Many will be called at this time when peace and healing occurs, and they shall rejoice in the name of God the Father. They shall be released from the bondage of sin and able to enter the Throne of grace, where they shall truly see the Father's face and hear his voice as he speaks to them personally.

They will then obey and become a new creation in Christ and will go about doing the Father's work here on earth as required. The Father and I long to see this time come to pass, as many will turn from their ways of sin and be once again restored to the Heavenly Father and myself.

Be still my child Rose of Sharon and know that it is I who writes these Letters that you are now typing. It is through God's Holy Spirit within you that enables you to hear these Words that I give you. Believe and it will be accomplished through you as you allow God's Holy Spirit to join with your human Spirit and lead you into all understanding.

Be of good cheer my child for it is an exciting time when many will truly know me as you have come to know us. Be still my child and fret not about things. I will give you the gift of peace in order for you to do the Father's work. Be not concerned about the things of the world that constantly surround you in your busy day.

Walk with me in the Garden of Eden and I shall show you the wonders of God's glorious hand upon the earth. He longs to show you personally and can only do so if you continue to believe and trust in him for all things, never allowing the doubts of Satan to enter into your mind or such doubts will destroy all that God is doing through you.

Stand up, be counted and know that God is with you, leading you, guiding you, and comforting you in all things. Go and tell the elders this Good News and many will begin to see God in a new and wonderful light.

Many shall shout out in Zion with praise and thanksgiving as they see the dawn of a new day rising. My love shall flow out as never before to comfort my people.

They shall hear my voice as a Shepherd gathers his sheep and shall be protected from Satan the evil one who seeks to devour their soul.

Many shall be consoled as I show them the new way. They shall then turn from their old ways and begin a new life in Christ as I begin to live in them. In this way, God's name will be proclaimed in all the land as many observe signs and miracles done in his name.

A time is coming soon when my people will gather together in my name and sing praises to God in Heaven who will see the hearts of his people and be glad. He will see the joy rising up from their faces and the love that will be shown to their fellowmen as his love flows through them to those around them.

Proclamation

Many shall be transformed in the name of Jesus Christ, and the Father, and they shall live a new life unto God. The former life will pass away and they shall begin a new life in Christ.

His people shall stand to witness and testify to those around them. Many shall see changes in their lives and shall come to see God and Jesus Christ much more clearly, with an understanding of all he has planned for mankind. Those who cry out aloud will hear his voice and they will be his people.

Many hearts will be changed and renewed as new wine is poured into new wineskins and the love of God shall flow through them into those who come into contact with them. By this many will be drawn to the Father and his glorious Throne.

The angels shall rejoice in Heaven as they see the changes here on Earth. Many will develop this special relationship and will know the Father as never before. They will call his name and he will hear their cry. He will make himself known to those whom he is drawing to his Throne and they shall truly see him as he is.

My love for my people is strong and I am here waiting for all who long to know and see my face. When they cry out to me I will answer their call and plea for help. I will give them the desires of their heart and they shall be filled with joy and gladness as they come to know me as I truly am.

I died so that they could have life Eternal and be reconciled to the Father, so that he could once again teach them all that they need to know. No more will they wander in darkness. No more will they cry out; for they shall know me and I shall know them.

Proclamation

It will be a time of much rejoicing as they develop and grow into the temple made by Holy hands. It is being fashioned and crafted into a beautiful temple which will hold the glory of God. When all the saints come together and worship as one, this temple of people will rise up in the air at the second coming of Christ, our Lord and Saviour and King.

Many shall be changed, in the twinkling of an eye at the Last Trump. We shall be caught up in the air with those who have gone before us and we shall be that Holy and perfect temple of God.

We shall be transformed into perfect Spirit bodies, new creations all fitting together perfectly as one unified body of Christ.

In this way we will fulfil the new Testament scriptures and Satan will be bound in chains of darkness where there will be weeping and gnashing of teeth.

Be still my child. Know that I am here right by your side throughout your journey here on earth. I am here to guide you and lead you and strengthen you in troubled times. Look to me for strength, guidance and wisdom and I shall give you all understanding to achieve all that I give you to do.

Be still my child and fret not, for I have conquered the evil one and he must flee at my name. Do not be frightened for I have overcome him and he knows that he has but little time left to upset these plans as they unfold. His hands will be bound up and he will be unable to touch those who have been set aside and sanctified by God.

But he will try to make war on those who remain. He will place anger, hatred and rage in their heart in order to stop the plan of God coming into action. Much bloodshed will occur as nation will rise up against nation and people against people.

My heart will yearn to comfort those who are inflicted with the pain that Satan will place in their heart, causing them to fight and destroy one another in vengeance. Much pain, sadness and sorrow will take place before they come to truly know the Lord their God. They will cry out to him in their misery and sadness. They will ask for rocks to fall upon them to rid them of this pain, but they must endure many more woes until my return as the Messiah, the King of Israel.

My love for my people will go forth and break the bonds that Satan has placed upon the earth, and my people will truly see me as I am and as the Father is. Many hearts will be broken and remoulded to form that perfect Holy temple without spot, blemish or wrinkle and they shall be a new creation beholden in the glory of God for all nations to see.

I will bring my people out from among them and they shall know that I am their Lord who has delivered them out of Egypt and into the Promised Land.

They shall cross over the Red Sea and shall enter into the place of rest, where they will be one with the Father. Here they shall see the Father as never before and shall enter into the Holy of Holies to approach his Holy Throne of grace.

Here they shall feel God's mighty hand upon them and shall be equipped with the fruits of God in order to do the work he requires of them. There will be much joy, gladness and singing of praise as his will is accomplished in each one of their lives and they come into that perfect harmony.

God's hand is upon his people to deliver them out of the depths of darkness. They will answer his call as he leads them up out of the darkness into his glorious light.

Proclamation

Many shall be transformed and they shall sing a new song unto the Eternal Lord. Their hearts will jump with gladness as they are washed clean in the blood of the Lamb, the blood of their Saviour and King. Their sins will be forgiven and they will be made white as snow to stand before the Eternal God in righteousness. They will sing praises from their hearts to God the Father and Jesus Christ, as they become new, spiritual creations in Christ.

Their human Spirit will join with the Father's Holy Spirit and they will be transformed and renewed like never before. Jesus Christ will live in them and they will live in him.

By this all men will know that they are of the Father. They shall see their good works and praise him (Matt. 5:16). They will be then drawn to the Father and seek to know him to be transformed as you are being transformed right now. Many shall be drawn to the light that will flow from your heart and you will lead many to the Father and his son. The Father can then teach them personally as they grow and change and become renewed by his love and Spirit, so that all will fit together in unity to the glory of God the Father.

Be still, my child and know that all will be accomplished in order to bring many sons and daughters to God's glory. Rose of Sharon, know that I have spoken all these Words tonight and that I will make the time available for you to type out all the Letters. Be of good cheer my child for the time is coming soon when God's glory will be revealed through you. Many shall see the transformation and give praise to God the Father, King of Kings and Lord of Lords.

Shabbat Shalom

LETTER 38

My Love Shall Fill The Void

Dearest child,

My heart yearns for peace to reign upon the earth as it is in Heaven. So many cry out for peace, but vengeance is in their heart. They know not the way of peace or how to obtain it. Many seek to know me and kill for my name's sake but they do not truly know me as I would have them know me.

I am the light and the way to peace and all who cry out to me with a broken and contrite heart will see myself revealed in them as never before.

My love and peace shall be poured out as they look to God the Father for wisdom and understanding and lean not on their own ways. They do not have the keys to Eternal life, as there is nothing but

bickering and fighting amongst my people. Oh how I long to be at one with each of them so that they can truly see me as the Father sees me and knows me.

Be still my child and listen carefully to all that I have to say. I am NOW revealing myself as never before. Now is the time when hearts will be opened up to receive all that I long to give them. The wait is over, and many shall rejoice as they truly see me and feel my presence within them. This will witness to their human Spirit and they shall walk with me in the Garden of Eden, where Heavenly peace reigns forever more.

At last the prayers of the people will be answered and I shall be incorporated in their very life and breath; in their everyday walk with God. I shall teach them all that they need to know and I shall lead them to that perfect place of peace and restoration. It is here that they shall rest their weary souls in order to be renewed and refreshed and rise up as eagles.

Here they shall lie down beside green pastures and feel my protective hand upon them. They will obey the Shepherd's voice when I call and they shall approach the Father's Throne to praise God's Heavenly name. They will rejoice because he is the Almighty King of all the Heavens and the earth and is worthy to be praised.

Be still my child and know that I have called you to spread the Good News of my love that is being poured out into the hearts of the broken, to be transformed into that perfect temple which will rise at my second coming. That perfect temple, unified by God's Holy Spirit, becomes as one and is fitly joined together in perfect unison.

Many shall see that perfect temple and long to be a part of it but shall be unable to, until God's Spirit transforms their hearts into a new creation.

Be still my child and faint not, for I am here in your midst and I shall give you strength to endure and courage to go and tell others of this Good News. They are searching and long to hear my messenger who shall proclaim the love that will be poured out across the nations. It is with great anticipation that my Father and I have waited for this day, as one by one people's hearts are changed and drawn to us.

It is indeed a time of much rejoicing as many shall know me intimately and experience everything and more of what you have experienced during our journey together. We live as one and I am in you and you are in me. My love now flows through your heart into those who seek to find me. As I send them to you, you will allow them to experience my love through all that you teach them, sharing your testimony and the hope that dwells within you.

Speak up and hold nothing back as I begin to open up their hearts and minds to receive the love I so desperately want to give to them, so they can also live in me and I in them. Peace my child, be not afraid. I am with you and shall guide, direct and carry you through as you proclaim the Good News.

All praise to God, our Heavenly Father and loving King of Kings. He is eagerly waiting to develop a special personal relationship with those whom he is drawing to his side. He so much yearns to know them and teach them the true way of peace, happiness and Eternal life.

My love shall fill the void that exists in their heart, just as I filled your void when you cried out to me in heartfelt prayer. I answered your call and your heart was transformed and renewed and you became a new creation for all to admire.

Your transformation has not gone unnoticed, by both the natural and the spiritual world. I want to warn you to always stay close to the Father and myself so as not to give the devil a foothold in your life. Look to me and I shall support and comfort you as you go through difficult and trying times.

My love will flow out and heal the hurts that many have in their hearts.

Their burdens will be lifted as they come to see us more clearly. Their lives will take on a new form as they become like us. The Holy Spirit will strengthen and lead them to myself and the Father, as we reveal ourselves through those around them. They will come together as one to worship, unified in one Spirit, even as my Father and I are one. They shall then be at peace and truly know me in the way that my Father knows me.

This is the plan of God: for all to come to him in worship, praise, prayer and devotion, living for him and his way of life. It is then that they will cry out "Abba, Father" and truly know him as I myself know him (Rom. 8:15).

This is a day of much rejoicing and celebration. The time has now come for my Holy Spirit of love to flow out like a river upon the earth to those who call upon his name.

I shall touch the hearts and minds of all who seek me and the Father earnestly. When they cry out; I will answer. When they seek me; I shall reveal myself. When they search to know me; I shall make myself known in their Spirit as never before.

This is a time of triumph over Satan the devil, whose presence shall be held back while my work is completed in the lives of those I am working with. He will not be able to touch those whom I have sanctified and set apart as my Spirit leads them to this place of peace. I long to lift up many on high to show them the Father and the love he has for all who cry out and yearn to be with him. At last the time has come when many shall be changed and transformed as their Spirit is lifted and illuminated by God's magnificent light.

There is no darkness within him and he is pure light. They shall sense his magnificent presence as they come to know the Father in such a deep, meaningful and personal way. The commitment to the

Father will be binding and they shall enter through my blood, the sacrificial Lamb, to become that perfect and spotless offering.

They shall become Holy and righteous in God's sight and then they will truly see the Father God and his magnificent Throne in Heaven. They shall look upon it in awe and wonder, realising the significance of their Saviour and the Father's love for them.

They shall then praise God's Holy name and cry out in thanks with supplications as they are renewed and restored to that place of perfect harmony. They shall enter into the Father's rest and wander no more. They will feel his mighty hand upon them as they are lifted into his arms to be protected and cared for, just as a Father would protect and love his children.

There will be much hatred upon the earth as Satan goes off to make war within the hearts of those who are left. Many shall suffer under his hand as they follow the desires of their hearts and minds and seek not after God the Father in Heaven. Much sadness, sorrow and suffering shall occur here on earth as each one wars against the other in order to get their own way. Tears will be shed as they turn their hearts away from the Father and seek after their own hearts' desires.

They live to satisfy the aching within their heart and will never enter my rest until they seek after God and his way of peace.

Laughter will no longer be heard as they endure many hardships and famines. Many shall resort to despicable practices in that terrible time and will think nothing of it in order to fulfil the desires of their own lusts. This will be a time of great turmoil and great woe as many shall be wiped off the earth in thousands at a time. Many shall perish, never having known God the Father and the love that he so desperately yearns to give to them.

They will be given a second chance at the second resurrection and shall then see the Father for who he really is. It will be a time of much rejoicing and happiness as many will see God the Father and myself like never before.

Love shall heal the wounds they carry in their heart and they shall be transformed and taken up to God's Throne to see him as he truly is. In this time many will honour God and sing psalms of rejoicing for peace will now reign in their hearts as never before. God's love shall flow through their hearts, opening up the way to Eternal life and all that God has in store for those who are obedient to his calling.

My child, I see your sadness at the suffering which must first occur to allow these people to enter God's rest. I too am saddened immensely at the prospect of many suffering under such torture and hardship, wishing there would be another way of peace, but they must first choose the way in which they want to go. I cannot force them. They must decide for themselves. As such, many will simply obey the lusts of their heart, which only leads to death and tragedy.

My way is life and victory, but they must decide for themselves the ways in which they want to go. It is with much hope and anticipation that all will come to the Father and myself, that they may taste the true peace that now lives within your heart.

Go and tell those whom I place upon your heart all that I have given you tonight. Be at perfect peace my child as my Spirit will strengthen you and deliver you from the evil one.

Go and spread the Good News of the wonderful new life that many can now enter. Never before has this been made available to so many in such a short space of time. The hour is nearly here when my perfect peace will reign in the hearts of many as they allow me to live in them and they in me.

Yes now is the time to tell my people of the amazing works that are happening in your life and that are about to happen in their lives as they come to know me. Peace my child, be renewed in my Spirit which I will send upon you while you sleep. I will strengthen you to do my Father's will, to bring many to his glorious Throne of grace and his intimate understanding.

Peace my child and fret not at this hour of the night, I am with you and shall make a way for you to endure. I know your heart, the love that you have for those around you and how much you desire for them to know me as you do. They shall know me as you do and shall be a testimony of my love for you. Peace my child, I am always with you and will never leave you nor forsake you.

Shabbat Shalom

— LETTER 39 —

It Is Through Belief That All May Enter

Dearest child,

Oh, how I long to be with you right now to experience the inner joy that you are feeling. I see your heart and know your happiness as you come to terms with all that has happened today. Your wait is at last over and we can both rejoice, for the time has come when many will indeed truly come to know my Father and I as we truly are.

I see how excited you are and know you have many questions regarding the Letters and Alpha & Omega Board Game®. All will be revealed as you seek to find me and the Father. We will guide and direct your steps and show you exactly how we want you to establish it all.

Your love for us grows every day and every time we walk together in the Garden of Eden. Be still my child and faint not, for I shall strengthen you to be renewed and rise up as an eagle. Rest awhile and renew your Spirit in the rivers of life as you become the new creation that we long for you to be. Be still and stand strong, allowing God's glory to shine through all that you do in order to bring many to God's sanctuary.

Go and tell them of all that has happened in your life and allow God's love to flow through you to those who seek after him. Many right now are calling out in my name, looking and searching for answers to the desires I have placed upon their heart. How can they know the answers unless they are told? Go and spread the Good News of my second coming. For all who truly seek God with a sincere and contrite heart will find him and come to know me personally as their Lord and Saviour.

Allow your love to flow freely to all I send your way. Allow them to come to know you and the changes in your life that have been brought about by me. In this way many will learn of the calling that I have upon their life and thus they shall also walk with me in the Garden of Eden.

Be still my child and fret not. I am with you always, leading and guiding you as you walk down the path I have laid out before you. I shall open the doors no one can close and close the doors no one can open (Is. 22:22). I will reveal myself through the writings I have placed upon your heart so that many can read of the miracles that have transformed your life today. My love for you is strong; stronger than you will ever know in this human lifetime.

At my second coming you shall truly see me as I am and you shall be glorified with me as the Father is also glorified. Allow my love to flow freely through your life and into those around you as you come to see them as I and the Father see them.

Do not judge them by their outward appearance but by their hearts, as you already do.

My love yearns to heal their aching hearts and answer their cries for help. I can only do this through my obedient servants who are being prepared right now to be instruments. They will bring many sons and daughters to my Father's table to celebrate the meal he has laid out before them.

All who are worthy may enter into this feast prepared by the Father through the blood of the Lamb. It is through his perfect sacrifice that many may come to know the Father in Heaven. This truly is the Good News of the Gospel and it is now the time for all to hear and come to the Father. He is ready and waiting to receive all who long to know him and hear his voice as he cries out to them in their darkness and pain.

My love will conquer all pain and wipe away the tears that have been shed.

No more shall they wander the streets looking for me for I shall reveal myself to them in a way that they will know it is I who is calling them. As a Shepherd gathers his sheep, so too will I gather my people who yearn to know me and who cry out for help daily.

My love will flow like a river that washes clean all the sins that stain my people. I shall unleash the chains that bind them up so that they may be truly free to worship the Father.

Praise and rejoice with the Eternal and Almighty God for he is King and supreme over all. All majesty and honour belong to God for Holy is his name throughout Heaven and all the earth. My Word shall go forth and many shall walk with me in the Garden of Eden as I teach them the way of my Father and his love for all mankind. He has not neglected my people but has heard their cry for help.

I will send my messenger to lead them out of the house of Egypt and into the Promised Land where I have prepared a place of rest. They shall then taste of the fruit that I have set before them and they shall be a new creation as I show them the paths which I want them to walk in.

It is through belief that all may enter and come to know the Father and myself.

Be still my child and reveal this Good News as I have given it to you. Spread it among my peoples and show them how they may be delivered from their bondage. No more shall they serve sin as their taskmaster. No more shall they wander aimlessly in the wilderness for I am now revealing myself and they shall see me by night and by day.

Look up to Heaven and you shall see the Father as he really is. He will lead you into the green pastures of peace that you long for. Your heart shall be renewed and lifted up as you turn your heart to him and he shall create in you a new heart; one that will allow the Father's love to flow through you and into those around you.

Be still my child and know that it is I, the Lord God, who is giving you all that you are writing. I want you to be my witness for my name's sake. Go and tell them of the Good News that you now know. Shout aloud to the Lord God for "vengeance is mine", and he truly shall repay all who besmirch his name (Deut. 32:35). Go and tell them of the coming events and allow my love to flow through your heart to those around you.

Allow God's love to comfort and uplift those who cry out, for truly now is the time for all to cry out. I shall reveal myself so that many may be saved and have Eternal life.

No more shall they wander and walk aimlessly in the wilderness for I shall be that pillar of fire by night and cloud by day (Exo. 13:21). They will be delivered out of darkness and into God's glorious light.

They shall leave their captivity and walk with me and the Father as we lead and guide them into all understanding. They shall be delivered, Israel my people, into the place I have prepared for them.

They will cross over the river Jordan and into the land of rest and peace (Deut. 12:10).

They shall truly know my voice when I cry out to them and shall wander no more through the desert. Rivers shall burst forth and the desert shall blossom with new rose buds as many hearts turn to my Father and me.

Be still my child and fear not. I shall give you the Words to speak to proclaim my message. Go my child and fret not for my hand is upon you. I shall lead you into all understanding as you seek to know me and the Father.

Shabbat Shalom

LETTER 40

Create A New Heart

My dearest child,

So long have I wanted to talk with you about the plans I have now set in motion. The time is NOW for many to come to me for forgiveness of sin and the beginning of a new and different life in Christ.

I long to live within all who cry out to know me and to do the will of my Father who sent me down here on earth to accomplish all that he desired of me to do. This enables yourself and many others to be able to approach his most Holy Throne directly; entering in through the blood of the Lamb.

They become a new creation under Heaven and their eyes and ears are opened to all that my Father and I have to teach them.

It is indeed an exciting time as you record my Words here on paper. Go my child and give these Words to those whom I place upon

your heart, in order to do the will of my Father in Heaven. Many sons and daughters will be drawn to glory, in allowing them to truly see the Father as he really is. I came that they may have life and life much more abundantly (John 10:10).

Be reassured that I am by your side leading you every step of your life in order to accomplish all that I have set out in you to do. My Father's will is being done here on earth as it is in Heaven and many shall cry aloud, rejoice and praise his most glorious name in Heaven as they come to truly know God the Father.

Be still my child and listen to all that I have to tell you. Know that I am moving upon the earth in and through the hearts of my people, drawing them together as they come to worship God the Father in Heaven.

Proclamation

They will come together and praise his name as many give their hearts to God and allow him to create a new heart within them. They will feel the very presence of God within them as they grow closer in an intimate relationship with him. His love will flow through them and heal all of the past hurts in their lives and they will be renewed, refreshed and lifted up with wings of eagles.

Be sure that my love is here on earth right now accomplishing all that my Father wills to accomplish in the lives of those who he has called and chosen at this time. They will hear his voice and know it is indeed God the Father who is drawing them to his very presence and Throne.

Cry aloud and shout out. For the time is now, for those to come into his very presence and come to know him as never before. He will directly lead and guide all who cry out to him and they shall hear his voice and follow as a Lamb follows a Shepherd. There will be much rejoicing and gladness as hearts are changed and transformed as never before.

My love will flow through the hearts of my people. Others around them will know that they are from the Lord as they see the works of their hands and see the changes in their lives as they grow in the grace and knowledge and wisdom of the Lord.

Praise and rejoice, for the Almighty is good and shall reign forever more. He is the Father of all who are upon this earth and has come to reclaim their hearts and draw them back to himself and his Throne.

This is indeed a time of much rejoicing and great gladness. Never has there been a time such as what is about to take place.

God's will and timing are perfect as he calls each person whom he has set apart and chosen. The Father draws each individual as he desires and they will be perfected according to his will and purpose as he prepares the temple to rise at my second coming.

They will long to see the Father and know him as you, Rose of Sharon, and I, now know him and they will grow, just as you yourself have grown over the past year. Be still my child as my perfect will is being accomplished in your life.

Yield to my Spirit residing within you and you will be taught and instructed in the way to live your life. Walk in the Spirit every day, allowing me to change and mould you into being that perfect vessel in which to hold God's glorious love.

Many will see the changes in you and long to know God as you have come to know him. Give them the keys to the Kingdom and allow them to also go to the Father and be changed forever in this life. Know that I have spoken these Words you have written here tonight and want you to go out and spread the Good News as you have received it from me.

Be at peace my child. My perfect will is being accomplished through your obedience. I am well pleased with your efforts so far and know the challenges that you face every day.

Rest in me my child, allow me to live within your heart and I will give you the desires of your heart to bring glory to God the Father.

Shabbat Shalom

LETTER 41

The Veil Is Removed

My dearest child,

I have come here before you today to tell you of the most blessed and wondrous things that are about to occur here on earth before your very eyes. My Father and I have longed for this time to come and now it is here.

Celebrate the coming of Christ, as I now live in and through the hearts of those we are drawing at this time!

My very essence is placed in each of those who long to know the Father and myself more intimately and as such I live in the very hearts of men and women here on earth. God's Holy Spirit flows out into all the hearts that are searching and seeking to know me, whose hearts are turned to submission and obedience to the Father and his way of life.

They are now a new creation under Heaven and as such are able to have a close and intimate relationship with the Father and myself as never before.

They will know me constantly and forever walk with me as I teach them the ways of my Father in Heaven. They will be strengthened to endure against the evil one and I will forever be their guide to lead them as a Shepherd leads his flock. They will hear my voice when I call out to them and they will answer and respond to do the will of my Father in Heaven. God so longs to know them and to reveal himself to them individually. He longs to teach them personally as they are changed inwardly and grow in the grace of God the Father.

His way is the way of life. Satan's way is the way of death.

There is no light in Satan or his evil ways, neither is there any darkness in the way of God the Father. The Father draws those whom he has chosen to be sanctified and set apart, for his purpose of leading others to him by their example and testimony. In this way many will be drawn to the Father and will come to see him as he really is; to know him intimately in a relationship, face-to-face.

This is indeed a time of great rejoicing and happiness as the veil is removed.

There will be great shouts of joy and gladness as many hearts are turned to the Father in a way like never before. At long last they shall see the Father as he really is and he will reveal himself to them in all his glory. The angels will shout and sing praises as many come to the Father and present themselves as living sacrifices.

They shall enter through the blood of the Lamb and become as righteousness in God's sight as they are changed and transformed into new creations.

Together raised as one Holy temple, perfect, unified and of one accord by the Holy Spirit.

Be still my child, and know that it is I, your Lord and Saviour who has spoken these Words to you. I know your heart and rejoice in the belief that you hold, which allows me to speak these Words to you through your open heart.

There is a time coming when all your family will know me as you yourself do. Be patient my child, do not weep or mourn, for soon this time will come. Weep not my child, for your heart's desire will come true. I long so much to give you the richness of my grace to allow you to see the Father in the way that he wants you to.

Fret not and be of good cheer for now is the time to open up your heart to all those around you. Judge not and let them see God's glory through your life and example. Let that be the testimony for all your friends and family to see.

I have placed various ones close by you to encourage and comfort you. Don't let Satan the devil get a foothold as you go about doing the Father's business.

There is much to accomplish by the will of the Father in Heaven and he is preparing a way for you to walk down the path of his choice and calling. Everything will be ready for you to achieve all that you need to achieve at the right time. My hand is upon you my child and I will lead you where it is I want you to go.

Be still and believe with all your heart the things that I tell you. Hold on to these things and remain steadfast in the meantime. Thank you for your labours so far, I will provide the time and opportunity to complete the Letters and move your heart to do all that I want you to do. Be still and worry not, for many hearts are now opening up to seeing me and the Father for the first time. They hunger and thirst for information as to how to approach the Throne of grace.

Go and tell them all that I have told you. Give them the Good News of the coming of Christ and of this new relationship they will develop with myself and the Father. This is indeed an exciting time that we live in. Satan knows he has but a little time here on earth so he will go off to make war with the remnant. Be not afraid little child for I shall not allow you or any others set apart by me to be hurt by the evil one.

Stay close to me in prayer, study and meditation and continue to put on the armour of God every day to be protected from the deceit of the evil one. His arrows go straight to the heart and if unprotected can undo the work that my Father and I are accomplishing through you.

Allow our love to flow freely through your heart and be healed by God's Holy Spirit. Put on the full armour of God to protect yourself daily and seek after God and his ways. He shall reveal himself as you take time to find him. He is calling you to a higher place and longs to show you the richness of his amazing grace and mercy as you allow him to transform your heart and mind.

Be lifted up into his arms and hide under the shadow of his wings. He will comfort and console you when you are downtrodden and discouraged as he knows your pain and suffering. He longs to wipe away your tears and produce tears of gladness. He loves and cares for you and all mankind on an individual level. His love is incomprehensible to the human mind and cannot be measured in human terms.

We both look forward to that great and glorious day when I shall return in all the glory my Father has bestowed upon me. I will meet with those my Father is changing and we shall rise and be together as one. Peace will reign on earth in this time to come and God's love will flow like a river. Many shall come and taste of the goodness, grace, mercy and forgiveness from the living water that is offered for all to drink.

God's hand is upon the earth and he is answering the prayers of the people as they cry out to him, so they shall be renewed and comforted as never before. He will bring them out of the land of Egypt and into a land flowing with milk and honey. He will guide them and lead them as they leave behind the slavery of sin and cross over into the river Jordan, to become a new creation and receive the new hearts that God so desperately longs to place within them.

They will be his people and know him as their "Abba, Father" (Rom. 8:15) crying out to him for help and protection from the evil one. God's hand will be on his people and he will lead them into a land of peace and tranquillity, not established by human hands.

They will become new creations under Heaven and shall know us as the Father and I really are.

Be still my child and know that this is the Word that I am giving you tonight. It is my prophecy of things about to occur here on earth. Much change is about to occur to the hearts of many around the nation. They will hunger and thirst to know the Father as they see others around them being changed and transformed.

Know that my Word is being proclaimed throughout the world as a witness to those who seek to know me and the Father. I am proclaiming my prophecies to various ones as a testimony of things to come. They will know it is of me when they read the Words you have written and will be convicted in their heart.

Be still my child and rest as I put my plan into action and show you all that I want you to do. Be open to change and to the things I want to place upon your heart. I will give you the opportunity to do these things as I know you lead a very busy life.

My love grows within you like a bud begins to bloom into a perfect rose.

This is a testimony of the love you have for my Father and me. I see your fears, hurts and your desires as you think of the coming year and all that I have planned for you and your family. Go my child and be of good cheer as you come to know the Father and taste of his glory.

Your love for me continues to grow as we develop a closer and stronger relationship. You are coming to know the Father and I as we long for you to know us. We look forward to the day when you will totally see the glory of my Father and receive the gift of Eternal life that is available to all who desire to know us.

Look forward to that coming day with joy and peace in your heart, as you become convicted of the love that I have for you and those I am calling at this time.

My child look up to Heaven and see the Father as never before. He longs to reveal himself to you. He knows everything about you and the love you now have for him in your heart. He knows the petitions of your heart and longs to comfort, console and care for you. He longs to remove the Spirit of heaviness and replace it with joy, peace and happiness.

Delight in him and he will give you the desires of your heart.

Your faith is strong and grows stronger every day as you hope for that day. Be still my child and fret not, that day will come soon when you will know him much more intimately and shall see him as he really is.

Do not listen to the lies of Satan for he wants to snatch away that joy and turn it into heartache, pain and suffering.

Do not listen to his half-truths and deceitful lies for he is the destroyer of all that is good and Holy. He longs to steal away your joy the minute you receive it in your heart. Always be on guard and don't let him infiltrate your heart and mind with lies. Be ye anxious for nothing and place your hope in the Lord; he will give you the things you long for in your heart.

Know that I am always here by your side and in your heart, constantly guiding and directing your paths in the way that you should choose. Follow the Spirit and allow me to direct your paths and I shall lead you into all happiness, and peace. You shall sit down in pastures green and drink from my abundant waters.

Fear not, for I have you and your family in my tender, loving care and I will not let you be hurt by the evil one. He is under the authority of my name and has to flee from your presence as you pronounce my name out loud. Be still my child, and know that I am with you always, even unto the end. My love will conquer all and reside in the hearts of those whom the Father is drawing. Go and tell them the Good News of this Gospel and of my soon return as their Lord and Saviour, Jesus Christ.

Shabbat Shalom

LETTER 42

Approach The Throne Of Grace With Confidence

My dearest child,

My love for you is such that you will never fully comprehend nor understand the vastness, depth or height. I have called you at this time to be a disciple of mine; to witness to those around you, of the love that now flows through your heart. Be still my child and be not afraid for I shall lead you into all understanding and give you the Words to speak when I require you to stand and give your testimony. In this way many shall come to know me and shall be drawn to the Father's Heavenly Throne.

Be still my child and fret not for all will be accomplished as my Word goes out as a witness to my people before my return to earth when the Father shall restore my glory here once again. It is then that every eye shall see me as I truly am and every knee shall bow as they come to know the Father and I as one. It is for this very purpose that I came to earth as a human; to bring glory to God the Father and bring many brothers and sisters to his side. Rejoice and be truly glad as the time draws near with each passing day. There is a new day dawning and the sun is rising to bring forth the Good News of my second coming here on earth.

The mountain shall rise and many will come unto it to learn more of God's way of life.

Salvation and Eternal life are now being offered to all mankind and many will see the Father and myself for the first time. There will be much rejoicing and gladness as they come to understand God's master plan for all mankind and the part the first fruits play in leading many others to his way of life.

My child I want you to listen as I speak these Words to you. I have a plan that I have set in motion and I want you to carry out the task as I reveal it to you. My Word is going out to the nations, as we speak, as I have called various children to record the Words I speak to them for all to see. I want you to type and copy all that I have given you and present it to the churches that send for you. They will hear my testimony through you so I need you to be prepared for when they call.

My light will then shine to those who now sit in darkness and my Word will be preached in preparation for my second coming. My love is guiding my people back to the Father and myself. It will comfort them as they learn of my way and the path they must walk down to receive grace, mercy, love and forgiveness from the Father.

In this way many shall hear of your testimony and be convicted as they themselves seek to understand how they may approach the Father's Throne. It is indeed an exciting time that we live in. We groan in anticipation of all those who will turn their hearts to us and allow us to create a new heart within them. They will begin to witness for themselves the changes you describe and will bear much fruit as they live their life in the fullness of God's grace, hope and peace.

You have so much to give to those whom I will send to you. Go and tell them of the new life that now resides in your mind and body and the love that now flows through your heart. My Words shall be a testimony for all who seek to find me and know me as their personal Saviour and King.

I died for all mankind so that they could have a personal one-on-one relationship with myself and the Father.

There is a new and wondrous time ahead as many shall have the veil lifted. They shall be able to approach the Throne of grace with confidence and without fear or trembling. My Father yearns and longs to show them the riches and fullness of his Kingdom and of the incredible love that he has for each and every one of them. We long for them to feel and know just how much love we have for them individually.

Much pain and sadness has passed and now is the time for celebration as you come to God the Father and Jesus Christ your Lord and Saviour. My love will lead and guide them into all understanding. They shall know my voice when I call out to them and shall follow in my footpath; showing others the way to the Father. My love shall be overflowing to wash clean all who bathe in its glory.

Be still my child and fear not for I have chosen you to stand up and tell all that has happened in your life. Tell them of the incredible miracles, the peace and joy that now reigns in your heart and the relationship that you have with the Father and myself. Tell them how they too can have this same relationship if they seek to have it. My love comes at a time when my people are crying out to truly know me in their hearts.

There will be many tears of joy as they experience the Father's love and healing of previous pain.

Be still my child and know that it is I, the Eternal Lord of Hosts, the Almighty King of Kings and Lord of Lords who speaks with you today. I am the way and the truth and all who seek to know me shall abide in me and I in them. Be still my child as my love flows out to those who thirst and truly seek to find me. Go and tell them all they need to know as they come to understand the love that I have for each and every one of them for I long to be with them and to show how much I care for them personally.

I died so that they could stand glorified by the Father in my stead; enabling them to approach the Throne of grace.

It is truly a special time as I reveal myself to all who call upon my name. I will accomplish this through my first fruits, whom I have chosen to show many the way to the Father and myself.

Lead them, Rose of Sharon, and they will hear your voice and obey. Many shall have direct access to myself and the Father as I begin to live within their heart and they abide in me. Take care not to let Satan the devil get a foothold as you proclaim the name of God. He is out to devour any unsuspecting person so you will need to stay close to me and be on guard daily.

Put on the full armour of God each day so as not to be affected by his fiery darts (Eph. 6:16).

My child, I am well pleased with your efforts so far and will lead and guide you always, never leaving your side. I will be constantly beside you night and day as you go about doing the Father's business of drawing many sons and daughters to him. Your work is about to begin and many shall be pleased to hear the Good News that you bring. Be of good cheer and do not fear as I am with you always and shall give you the Words to speak. Be bold my child and teach them of the love that is being offered to each and every person who longs to know me and the Father.

Shabbat Shalom

LETTER 43

Enter Into God's Glorious Throne Room

My dearest child,

I am the Lord and Saviour whom you call upon by name. I am here as we speak to one another and I will show you the way. I will lead and guide you to the places where I wish you to go and will be by your side as you share your testimony with my people. I am drawing many back into my fold at this time and I want you to be a witness of things that are about to take place in the near future.

How will they know unless I send my messengers to tell of all that is to occur?

Be still my child. I see your anxiety and shall prepare a way for you to speak wherever I lead you. I will also place my helpers there so that you will be supported as you go to my people. Be not afraid for my Spirit will be upon you and I will put the Words into your heart to speak as you give your testimony. In doing so you will bring many sons and daughters to glory as they are drawn back to the Father's side, by accepting my sacrifice and asking me to be their personal Saviour.

I will support you always and will never leave you stranded. Be bold and take heart, as I shall give you the Spirit of boldness you have asked for. My peace shall be upon you and the joy of the Lord shall be your strength, as you reveal my Father and I to them, as we truly are.

You have come to develop a close and personal relationship with me and the Father and this is what we desire for all mankind. This also is the very essence of the board game that I have inspired you with, to allow many to play it and develop this relationship, becoming aware of the calling that I have placed upon them.

Stay close to me always and I shall take your hand as you enter each church that asks for you to come and give a testimony.

Stand up and give an account of how we have transformed your life from death to life, from darkness to God's most glorious light.

Proclamation

All praise to him who is our Lord and Saviour God. Rejoice in his mercy and grace as we see him face-to-face. Come and let us taste the goodness he longs to pour out upon those who seek him. He has many marvellous and wondrous blessings to pour out to those who truly wish to know him and be led by his Spirit. He is there constantly to comfort, teach and guide us in the way he wants us to go.

Be still my child and listen to my voice as I speak of the wondrous things ahead that I have planned for you. Know that my hand is upon you and I will keep watch over you always as you obey all that I ask. My will is being accomplished in your life and God's glory will be revealed to those around you as you lead them to that place of peace and harmony, a place of happiness and rejoicing.

Their soul shall never thirst as they come to the Father and drink of his Word and all that he has planned for those who come unto him.

They will hear his voice and answer his call and shall truly become as one with us. Their lives will change as they live their life in obedience to all that we show them.

My love shall heal their hurts as they become a new creation in Christ. Many will approach the Holy of Holies and enter into God's glorious Throne room to praise and worship him with great shouts of joy. There will be much rejoicing in Heaven as one by one, hearts are transformed. I will dwell within their hearts and cause them to live a new way of life.

Be still my child and fear not. I will give you the strength and wisdom to speak all that I want you to say. It is by my Spirit that you will be able to accomplish all that I want you to say and do. I will give you the Spirit of boldness and you will know it is I, your personal Lord and Saviour who speaks through you to my people. Let them see the new life that you now live and the peace and joy that now lives within your heart. My heart rejoices with you as you lead many to a new hope and life in Christ. God's Word will go out to the nations and my people will hear my voice.

When they see the testimony of your personal life they too will be convicted and drawn back to the Father's side. Then they shall taste of the wonderful blessings he wishes to share with each and every one of those whom he is calling at this time. I will strengthen you and give you the peace to accomplish all that I want you to do. Be still and trust in me to answer your heart's desires. I shall surely answer your prayers and the petitions of your heart as it is the Father's will and desire for me to do so.

I am your Lord and Saviour and I have come to give you life and life much more abundantly (John 10:10). Be still as I lead and guide you to the place where I want you to go. Stay in perfect peace and do not worry about what to say or about what others will think, just look to me and speak from your heart as I give you the Words to speak.

Shabbat Shalom

LETTER 44

Put That Belief Into Action By Doing

My dearest child,

Be still my child and look to me. I will give you the strength that you are looking for.

Do not look to man for approval, but to the Lord your God.

I am with you day-by-day, hour-by-hour, constantly leading and guiding you. Never forget the things I have shared with you and know in your heart that I have given you these Words personally.

My child, I need you to look to me and learn. Read the Scriptures daily so as to be filled with my Word so I can teach you of my ways and lead you in the path I want you to go.

Don't turn your heart and your head away from me in sadness, for I am the only way to inner fulfilment, peace, happiness and joy.

I see your reluctance as you listen to those around you who do not believe it is I, your personal Lord and Saviour. Be strengthened and know that it is I who writes these Words and not you as many would like to believe. I am using these Letters to draw many back into the fold, back to our Father God in Heaven as he draws them.

Be still and know that I am your Lord and personal Saviour. I have died so you could live. Live your life as I live within you and help you to become a new creation, destined since the beginning of time. I see the constant hardships you face on a day-to-day basis. But I will strengthen you for my hand is upon you. I will achieve all that I want to achieve in your life.

Be still and look to me. Fret not but be glad of heart, as the time is nearing soon when you will sing praises and rejoice as God leads you into his Holy presence. Know that I am guiding you as we speak, in order to lead you back into the Father's presence once more. My love is upon you my child and I will give you the desires of your heart as you cry out to us for help. We will be by your side to comfort you through this difficult and trying time.

Be still and enjoy the peace from my Father in Heaven, as he leads you back into his most Holy presence again. He is calling you at this time to his most Holy Throne, so that he may teach you and shower the love that he has upon you. Stand strong and know that I have overcome the enemy and he will flee from you when you cry my name aloud, as you have been doing.

My child, my child, look up to me and I will strengthen you and give you the desires of your heart. Look to me and I will give you the peace that you cry out for. My love continues to surround you and your family as you grow closer to me and the Father.

His love will be poured out to all the nations around the world as the sea covers the earth.

Many will call out to him and their hearts will be turned. You are right in saying that so many need to come to God. They do not know the happiness, the true happiness, which can be theirs if they just ask.

Be still and I will comfort you and give you the love and the peace that you desire. I know you believe in your heart that I can, so now put that belief into action by doing.

Spend time in prayer and meditation and reading my Word so that I can teach you and strengthen you with God's Holy Spirit. He will help you to endure all that you must suffer for my name's sake.

Be of good cheer and know that I am your Lord and Saviour and I am calling you to be my maidservant in order to lead many back into the Father's presence.

It is for this purpose that I came to live and die on earth; to release all mankind from the penalty of sin. By releasing them of this penalty, they were then able to enter God's Heavenly Throne of grace and become white as snow through the death that I suffered here on earth. It is God's desire that all may enter into his presence and be as one with the Father, myself and the Holy Spirit. Then they shall truly see the Father in all his glory and radiance and beauty that constantly surrounds him. All praise and thanksgiving belongs to him for he is great and greatly to be praised!

He longs to teach every one of us of the riches of his Kingdom. He longs to shower you with gifts of every kind and to lead many back into his wonderful presence. My love now awaits all who seek to find the Father, and I will be there to help them and show them the way to true happiness, peace, love, and fulfilment. It is then that they will be as one, as they accept me as their loving Saviour and God. I will live within them and they will know the Father in Heaven.

My love will guide them and lead them back to the Father as it is poured out through the hearts of those who yearn and seek after God. They will be my disciples and I will protect them as it pleases my Father in Heaven to comfort and draw many into his Holy presence. Be still my child and fear not, as I am leading you to that place which is being prepared right now as we speak. Great things are about to take place as doors open to allow you to do the Father's work and glorify God in my name.

Be still and know that my hand is upon you as you sit here and type out these Words I give you. I know that you do believe it is me and that you want so much to teach others of the wonders that my Father in Heaven has for all who look to him.

The time will come when they also will receive the gifts from Heaven and will become as one. God's love will truly flow through each and every one of them as they cry out and look to God the Father. In this way he will create a temple for many to learn of God's ways and they will be filled with his Spirit.

Be of good cheer and fret not. I know your sadness and heartache at this time as I lead you to that place where I want you to go. Much sadness and heartache will soon turn into much happiness and joy. You will see the Father's hand upon your life as you lift your heart to me in praise and thanksgiving. We will give you the love, peace and the comfort you so desire. Be still my child and know that I love you very much and care for you deeply. My hand has not left your side and will be forever leading you as you turn your heart and desires to me.

Be of good cheer and fret not, for I have come so that all may enjoy the love that my Father longs to give to all who cry out for it in his name. Be that example for others, that they may admire God's work in you, so that you may truly be that light for others to see. It is then that they will begin to glorify the Father in Heaven as they see the person that you are now becoming. Look to me, my child and I will show you the glory in Heaven as never before. We long so much to guide you into all understanding, knowledge and wisdom as you begin to lead and guide those around you.

There is much that we long to teach you as you live the life that my Father and I have for you. Be still my child and be of good cheer for the time is coming when you will see the Father and myself as never before and will feel our presence in your life in a strong and powerful way. Be at peace and look to us and we will give you the desires of your heart. The love you have for us is good, for we see your heart and know how much you long for my return.

I am coming soon and will be pleased to find my servants here on earth doing the work of the Father.

Shabbat Shalom

LETTER 45

Enter Through To The Holy Of Holies

My dearest child,

Take heart my child, I am forever with you and my love for you is endless. Be still and listen for my voice when I call out to you. Be not afraid for I am with you always, leading and guiding you as you turn your heart to me and God the Father. I am well pleased with your efforts so far and see how much you want to complete the board game totally.

I will provide the way for you to achieve this and you will know when the time is right. My child, I see the anxieties in your heart as I lead you through this present age. Know that my hand is forever with you and I have never left you. Continue to look to me and study my Word to be spiritually nourished and well-fed. This will strengthen you to become strong in faith and to understand all that I have planned for you and your family.

Be aware that Satan is lurking about and ready to steal your joy away from your heart. Do not let him in. Stand still and be strong. Be of one mind and be at peace as I show you the wonders of Heaven above. I am slowly revealing all that we wish to share with you and those who yearn to seek the Father in Heaven.

My heart is turned towards all who seek the Father and long to know him more deeply and personally.

Please guide and direct those whom I send to you and show them the new way of life that you have found and the joy and peace that now reigns in your heart. My love will flow out into those that come into your life so that they may taste of the Heavenly gifts my Father has for all who cry aloud to him in praise and worship. My love shall heal the hurts and pains they carry in their heart and you will reveal to them the key to releasing the weight of sadness. They hunger to know more and long to be filled as you are, so lead them to the waters that flow in abundance and they shall also receive the peace and love that you now experience.

Be still my child, Rose of Sharon, and know that I am the Lord God most high, who writes these messages through you to be given to those whom I am calling. There is much to accomplish and much to do throughout all the nations of the world. The time is now to show my people the love that now reigns in your heart and how your life has been transformed and changed.

Go and tell them all that you now experience so that they too may receive peace, love, mercy, forgiveness and grace. The way is being made clear for all to enter and come into the fullness of Christ. I am now revealing to you that a new day has dawned and the way is made clear for all to enter.

Whosoever calls upon the name of God for the forgiveness and redemption of sin will receive salvation and Eternal life. The time is now, for many to enter through to the Holy of Holies as they accept my sacrifice and are washed whiter than snow.

Prayer

Our Lord God on high, how much we thirst after you. We long to know you with our whole heart. Please teach us the way to peace and all understanding. Please guide us to the Father's Heavenly Throne so that we may be as one with him and yourself. We cry out to you Heavenly Father to wash us clean with the precious blood of the Lamb so that we may see you face-to-face once more. We long to be within your beautiful presence, oh Lord, to experience all the joys that Heaven longs to shower upon us. You bring much love and light into our lives.

Please, Father, show us the way to your Heavenly Throne that joy may reign in our hearts once more. To taste of the Heavenly fruits that you wish to give to each one of us who cry out to you, so that we may do the work here on earth that you wish for us to do, to lead many to your side. To bring many to your table as you draw each one of them. We long to experience your grace, mercy, peace and love as you show us the way to becoming a new creation. The love that you have for us is without measure and you so much long to show us just how much love you do have for each of us who cry out to you. Amen.

Take heart little child, for I am here right now by your side leading you as you look to us in your heart. My hand is upon you and I will continue to teach you as you search the Scriptures daily. Be not afraid for

I shall give you the boldness to speak. They shall see the changes in your life and be encouraged by all that you say. Know that my hand is forever upon you as you journey through your life, leading many to the Father's side. Well done and stay close to me as I teach you the wonders that await your discovery as you lean your heart toward me.

My peace I leave with you, my peace I give to you. Know that I am the Lord your God who loves and cares for you very much. Be of good cheer and turn your heart to the Father and myself, and we will give you the desires of your heart (Ps. 37:4).

Shabbat Shalom

LETTER 46

There Is A New Day Dawning

My dearest child,

My love for you is very strong and I am leading you into all understanding. Be still and wait upon the Lord for he shall answer when you cry out to him.

    My child listen carefully to all that I have to say. My Word is being preached throughout all the nations as I speak and I have much that I wish to tell you. Be of good cheer and wait upon the Lord for I am preparing many hearts for my soon coming return. Many shall cry out and I shall answer their call. Know that the love I have for each and every individual upon this earth is great and I long to lead them all into that place of peace.

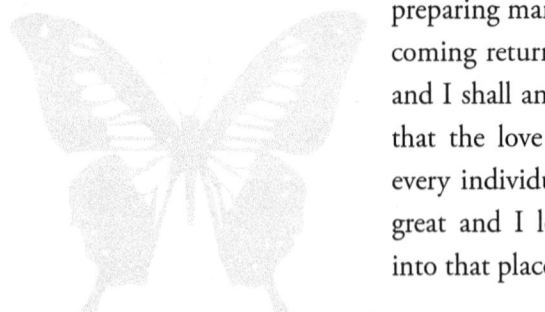

They do not know me, nor do they even seek me for they think they are rich, but they are poor. They think they have want of nothing but their lives are empty and meaningless and hold no hope. I am their hope and salvation. I am the way to Eternal life and happiness.

There is no other name under Heaven by which any can enter to receive the gift of Eternal life (Acts 4:12). Many are misled to believe they have no need to seek my name and that they are sufficient in themselves. They are unaware of the hold that Satan now has upon their lives. He has blinded them to their need to have a personal Saviour. He continues to deceive through the blindness that now surrounds them continually so they cannot see me nor know me.

My Word will go out to try and bring them to this awareness. They will hear but heed not. They will laugh and scoff at the Words that are spoken and ridicule the messengers that cry out aloud all that I have planned for mankind.

Be still my child and hear my voice as I prepare a message to go out to all people upon this earth. I am the Lord your God who is now at the right-hand side of the most high Father.

I am making ready for my soon coming return as I prepare the hearts of my people to receive me.

Listen and heed all that I say as I now tell you the wondrous things that are about to take place here on earth. Be still and know that I have called you to proclaim the Gospel and the Good News of my soon coming return. The hearts that I am preparing will carry out all that needs to be accomplished as the way is made ready for my second coming.

Many have sought to find me in the surrounding churches and many have been disillusioned and left. Many have been hurt and still carry the scars in their heart toward me. These very hurts stop many from seeing myself and the Father. They carry hurts that need to be healed so that they can see the way clearly to the Father in Heaven and all that he has planned for them and the love he longs to pour out into their hearts as he leads each one individually to his side.

Be still my child and fret not, for the time is coming soon when they will hear and understand all that my Father and I wish them to know.

My love will be poured out upon them as I heal the hurts that scar their hearts.

We anticipate this time as they begin to see us in a new light. No more will their understanding be clouded and far removed, for they shall see the Father and myself as never before. They shall experience a close and intimate relationship with us as we lead them into all understanding. The light will shine brightly all around them as they witness the Word going out into all the land, as many turn their hearts towards God the Father and accept me as their personal Saviour.

Be still and hear my voice as I tell you all that I want you to do. I see your anxiety as world events occur around you. Know that my hand is upon the current events and I am allowing these things to occur as I bring many sons and daughters to glory. They will seek me and cry out to me as they come to know me more intimately and personally.

Be still my child and cry aloud all that I have done and am doing in your life. Tell them of the wonders you now know and the love that you now have flowing through your heart. Know that my will is being accomplished in your life as you submit your ways to me and live your life in obedience to the Holy Spirit.

Be still my child and hear my voice when I call. Know that I am revealing to you all that is about to occur upon this earth as I make ready for my coming return.

My name will be proclaimed throughout all the land as a witness of my coming return.

Many will yearn to know me and will seek to find me to heal the hurts that they carry within their hearts. It is with great joy and gladness that I wait for the day when many will cry out to me, for I shall heed their call and answer their cry.

Much love shall I pour out upon them and they will know that the Lord their God has answered their heartfelt prayers. I will be there to lead and guide them to the place of peace and tranquillity. I will wash them clean of their sins and they shall be as white as snow.

No more shall they wander searching and seeking for me for I shall reveal myself and the Father as they turn their hearts to me. My love surrounds all who seek to know me. I shall free them from the hold that Satan has upon their lives and they shall see me clearly. I will live in them and they shall live in me.

It is the destiny of man to be at one with his maker.

It was destined from the beginning until sin was found in him. I am now drawing many first fruits to God's table to partake of the gifts that his most generous hand has to offer. Many will be changed and transformed and will show others of the wonders that he is now doing in the sons and daughters of those who believe in his name and cry out to him. Many will at last come to know the peace that I have from the Father and shall experience the true inner joy that was meant for all from the very beginning.

It was my Father's wish that all men and women would enjoy a life of enjoyment, happiness and fulfilment, free of sadness and pain.

The lives that we now lead are in contradiction to God's way of life. Happiness can only occur when sin is banished completely from the world that we now live in. This will occur in the end times as Satan and his demons are locked away, and will no longer be able to deceive all who live here on earth. No more sadness and pain, no more suffering or shame. Lives will be changed as people are liberated to seek God the Father and myself. True inner joy and peace will be found as many become transformed and recreated in the Father's image.

His magnificent beauty and splendour will now illuminate through each one who is willing to give his or her heart totally to God. Only then can he mould, shape and craft it into a new and beautiful creation. His laws will be written on their heart and they will come to know God in such an intimate and special way. They will yearn and seek to do his will as they become transformed and recreated. They will display fruits of his most precious Holy Spirit as it flows through them and permeates the lives of those around them.

By this all men shall know that they have been sanctified and set apart by God as they see the changes in their lives. They will grow in abundance as the day approaches.

So too will many reject and scoff at what is spoken and will continue to live a life of emptiness and sorrow. In their bitterness and hard-heartedness they will be unchanged and unmoved to seek God and will make life very difficult for those around them who seek to do so.

Be still and know that I am your Lord God and Saviour. My return will bring many to repentance and every knee shall bow before me when I return as King of Kings and Lord of Lords. Be still and know that there is a new day dawning. We approach that glorious day when every eye will see, and every heart will know the things that God the Father has for those who love him and keep his most precious commandments; that is, to love your God with all your heart and love your fellowman as you love yourself (Mark 12:30-31). By this all men shall know the true disciples and true followers of God (John 13:35).

Be still my child and be not afraid for I see your heart and know how anxious you are about the end time events. I see how much you love your family members and long for each one of them to come and know the Father and I as you do. This will come about as time goes on and you will see the glory of God upon each one of them as they are changed and transformed. Be sure that I am leading each one to the Father as he draws them to his side. My Word is being proclaimed and will show many the way.

Be of good cheer my child for the time of rejoicing will soon be here. Many will shed tears of joy as they come to see the love that my Father and I have for those who cry out and call upon his name.

Many will discover true peace and inner tranquillity as they live a life led by the Spirit and not by the natural desires of man. My love shall heal the pains and hurts that many have carried for a lifetime.

No more shall they hunger. No more shall they thirst. No more shall they want, for I am the bread of life. I am the way. I am their hope and salvation and shall lead many to the Father's Throne where they shall see him face-to-face. My love will forever surround them and lead them to become that new creation that God so longs for them to become.

My love will lift them up to the heights as an eagle takes flight and soars high above the earth. They shall be one with God, myself and the Holy Spirit. They shall wander aimlessly no more. They will have life so much more abundantly.

Every good gift under Heaven will be poured out upon those who seek to do God's will in their lives. They will be blessed abundantly as they come into a close and intimate relationship with God the Father. Be sure that I have chosen you to proclaim this Good News and to tell them of the miracle that is now being manifested in your life.

Shabbat Shalom

LETTER 47

I Hurt To See You Hurting

My dearest child,

My child, my child, Rose of Sharon, why do you turn your head away from me? I sought to speak with you but you ignored me. Why have you cast me aside and not listened to my promptings?

Please do not be angry towards me, as this allows Satan the devil to set a wedge between us. He would so much like to devour your soul and consume you in his fire of hatred and rage.

There is no light within him, nor will there ever will be. Do not allow him to consume your thoughts and your life. Turn to me wholeheartedly and I will lift you up and allow you to see the light and all that the Father and I have for you to partake of.

My child, seek me wholeheartedly and I will answer when you call out. Do not be despondent about the cares and worries around you—

look to me and I will deliver you from the darkness that surrounds you. Trust in me and I will deliver you from the cares that constantly consume your thoughts and attention.

Seek ye first the Kingdom of God and the way will be made known to you.

Allow me to enter and live once again in your heart. Allow me to empower you with the fruits of peace and goodness, love and gentleness, patience and long-suffering, faith, meekness and hope.

I will bring back the joy that you so long to have. You have mistakenly wandered away from the Shepherd's care and need to be brought back into the fold to be protected from the evil one at all times.

Peace my child and know that I am now leading you to that beautiful place of rest and love, where you can sit by waters still and be led to green pastures to be fed and cared for. Look to me always and be not discontented with your current circumstances. I have everything under control and the Father will lead you as the time is right and show you all that you need to know. Listen to the Holy Spirit when he speaks for he will guide you into all understanding and teach you all that you need to know.

My child take heart; you are very near and dear to me and I hurt to see you hurting, lost, lonely and sad. I died so that the way would be made clear for you to return to the Father and become one. Seek us with your total heart, mind and body and we will reveal ourselves as never before.

Place us first on your list of things to achieve and we will reward your efforts while you are transformed into the beautiful butterfly that we long for you to become. It is not through any works of your own, but by total submission to God the Father and me.

We will lead and guide you through our Holy Spirit as he moulds and develops your most precious heart. Look to us my child and we will complete the job that we have already begun in you. You will see the works of the Father in your life as you become transformed and renewed.

Many will see these wonderful transformations as they look upon you and remember you from before. They will not believe the changes in you and will ask questions about the hope that now lies within your heart. Be bold and tell them everything that I put within your heart to say. They will hear the Words and know that God the Father has had his hand upon you and achieved the changes in your life. In this way your personal testimony will lead many to him as they ask you the way to the Father's presence.

My child I am so pleased to see that your heart has at last turned around and you have begun to search us once again with all your heart, mind and soul. We long to teach you so much so that you in turn can teach those whom we send to you. The Letters that you type, Rose of Sharon, will bring many sons and daughters to glory at the right time, as they read your personal testimony on paper and see the transformation of your life.

Be of good cheer my child, for I am here right by your side to lead and comfort you as you walk the spiritual walk that I direct you on.

Look to me always and be not afraid for I have overcome all that you fear. I have defeated death and now live at the Father's right hand in his most glorious Heavenly abode.

Be still and listen for my voice when I cry out to you. Be bold and stand up for me whenever the need arises and I will stand up for you in the Heavenly realms and guard you against the evil one when he asks for you by name.

Shabbat Shalom

LETTER 48

Seek Me First

My dearest child,

I see the tears that you shed as you type this letter. Be still my child, I am with you, leading you and guiding you into all understanding. Be patient and wait upon the Lord and he will lead you as a Shepherd leads his sheep. Be at peace my child, do not be dismayed or alarmed at the things you see around you for I have conquered sin and now sit at the right side of the Father's Heavenly Throne, waiting for the time of fulfilment when I shall return to earth to rescue my people from the clutches of sin and death.

The way to your heart has been made clear and now I am able to communicate directly with you. So, too, am I waiting to communicate directly with all mankind and to have them look to me for teaching, wisdom and all understanding.

My will is to live in the hearts and minds of all men and women upon this earth as they look to me as their Saviour, Lord and King.

I will deliver all who cry out to me and call upon my name and I will reveal myself to all who seek to know me personally. Listen carefully my child as I teach you of the wonders from Heaven. Be still and hear my voice in all earnestness.

My love will flow abundantly to cover the earth as never before known to mankind.

I am preparing the path for many to enter, who call upon my name as they seek to find me in their hardships and trials. Be still my child and look to me for strength at this time of testing. I know how much your heart longs for this to occur in all people who are hurting here on earth. Be assured that this will happen and you will help to spread the Good News of my soon return.

Many will hear and answer the call in their heart as my Father draws them to his side.

He longs to be at one with each and every one of them. He longs to show them the love that he has for each and every one of them personally. Do not be deceived and misled by Satan the devil. Satan longs to lead each one away from the love that the Father wants to share with each and every one of those whom Satan is drawing away at this time.

Please do not become discouraged or lose heart for the time is drawing near when you will be called upon to stand up and give an account of everything that has happened to you and the new life that you now live as I live in you and you live in me. Show them the fruits that are now being produced in your life as a personal testimony of my love flowing through you.

Know that I have placed my Spirit within you to become transformed and changed into a beautiful butterfly, attracting many to the beauty that you now hold within your heart.

I know how much you long for your family members to experience the same joy you do and by your very example you will lead many to that place. My hand is upon each one of them, bringing them to a place where they will see my hand in their life. Each one will seek to find me and I will answer them in their tears of sorrow, pain and hardship. They will rejoice as they too discover the love that I have for each one of them and they will feel the very presence of God within their lives and in their hearts.

Be still my child. I see your sadness and the tears that you cry. Don't give up or become discouraged for I have seen your heart and will answer you as you totally commit your life to me. Be of good cheer, be not afraid, for my Word has been spoken and I will allow it to come to pass as you draw closer to me in prayer and study. Seek after me wholeheartedly and I will lead you to that place of peace and tranquillity once again.

Know that I have all things in order in Heaven and on earth and my will is being accomplished. Take heart. Do not be dismayed or disheartened when you do not see things happening as quickly as you would like them to. I am preparing the hearts of my people and as they turn their hearts to me I am able to accomplish all things.

Seek me first my little one, and all things will be accomplished as I have said.

Believe as you have done, continue to worship the Father in Heaven and praise his most glorious name and you will see the beauty that now surrounds you in Heaven and on the earth. My Father longs to teach you so much and I know that you have a willing heart, ready for the things he has prepared for you. In order for you to stay close to him continually, seek after him first and foremost and do not neglect his teachings.

Be assured that Satan the devil is prowling around like a lion and longs to take you away from the Father's Heavenly Throne. DO NOT LISTEN TO HIS LIES! He is deceitful above all things and longs to steal away the joy which now reigns within your heart.

Stay close to me and drink of my Word as I teach you all things. Read and I will give you insights and revelation.

Take this revelation and go and tell my people that they too may learn this teaching. Be still and know that I am here constantly to lead and carry you through all that you need to endure for my name's sake. Trust in me and believe that Heaven and all its glory will open up to you as you draw your heart closer to me.

Shabbat Shalom

LETTER 49

Spirit Of Power

My dearest child,

I love you very much. My little one, be still and listen for my voice as I speak the Words I wish to give to you tonight. Be ye not afraid of the things that are about to take place. Know that my hand is upon you and your family and I will lead you step-by-step as you venture through life here on this earth. Be still my child and be of good cheer. Hope will be forever there to guide you as you lead many to the Father's Throne and to his beautiful way of life.

I look to you to continue in accomplishing the Father's good works in glorifying his most Holy name. The tool *Alpha & Omega* will lead many to a better, clearer understanding of how to come before our Heavenly Father. So many yearn to know him more clearly and they will see his hand upon their life. So many are searching and seeking and know not the way to find him. Many will come to this understanding as they read the *Letters* I have given you and also play the board game that I have led you to create.

Much joy and gladness will result in many coming to see the Father and know him as their very own God. So much happiness and healing will result as many are cleansed of their sins and the way is made clear before them. Be of good cheer and look to the fruits that they will bear once they have truly given their life to God the Father in Heaven.

Proclamation

Many will shout aloud with praise and thanksgiving as they commit their life to Jesus Christ their Lord and Saviour and the Almighty, Eternal Father God in Heaven.

My child, hear my voice as I speak to you tonight. Do not let the seed of doubt grow in your heart. Stomp it out quickly before it gets any foothold. The Words I speak to you, they are life, and will give life to anyone who seeks to read them. I know your heart and how much you love your fellowman and how much you long for them to come to know us as you have done. I also long for the day when every heart will know God in this way. Stand strong and be of good cheer.

You now have the gift of peace in your heart and many will witness this and see the changes in your life through your actions. Be still and hear my voice when I call aloud to you. Follow the Spirit as he leads you day and night. Be forever open to where he will lead you, and be obedient and willing to follow.

Do not be afraid and shrink back in fear for I have given you a Spirit of power and will give you the strength to continue. Be not afraid of what man thinks about you but stand up and be glorified by my Father in Heaven as you speak his name boldly. Continue to tell them about the changes that have happened to your life and how you have been changed and transformed. Be of good cheer my child and know that all will go well. Rest and look to me for I will give you the desires of your heart as you come closer to me and God the Father.

Shabbat Shalom

LETTER 50

Total Heartfelt Commitment

My dearest child,

My child, continue always to look to me. Never take your eyes off me, not even for a minute. I love and care for you deeply and will see you through your journey as you venture through life and all that I have planned for you.

My Word and the Good News of my soon return is going out and being witnessed to the nations around the earth. Many seek to know me personally, yet do not know how to find me. I want you to show them the way.

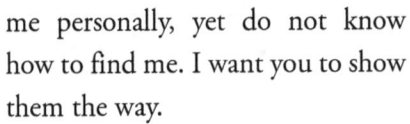

Show them how you are able to go to the Father's Throne in worship and in prayer.

Show them how you have become a new creation in Christ, and

of the love that now flows within your heart. Reveal to them the intimate and close and personal relationship that you now know in your heart, mind and Spirit.

Many cry out to me daily to know the way and they yearn for the peace that now surrounds you. Show them the way and lead them to the Father in order for them also to learn of the wonderful Heavenly gifts that lie waiting for them also.

My child, Rose of Sharon, I am fashioning you for a particular purpose and would like you to share these deepest and most personal thoughts and feelings in order to draw many back to the Father. Speak of the joy that now lives within your heart. Show them the love that flows out to those who surround you and the miracles that have occurred in your life as you have devoted your life to God the Father.

My child, be assured that I will tell you the right time to act and to speak and to carry out the wishes of myself and the Father. Do not be concerned with these things but rest in my peace, reassured with the hope that now lies within your heart.

Continue to be of good cheer and cry out aloud in praise and worship to God the Almighty and loving Father, whom we all worship and adore. Be forever in awe of his incredible majesty and beauty and Holy presence. Know that he is and was and is to come, always and Eternal, forever and ever, Amen.

Prayer

Our Father, whom we love and adore, peace be upon all your people who now worship you here on earth. Draw us, Father, closer to your side as we come to worship you in prayer and praise. Be forever merciful with the faults that we commit and forsake us not when we are deep in our iniq-

uity, but deliver us up out of evil and show us your true, beautiful and pure light from Heaven.

Show us the way to your majestic Throne and reveal in us your true purpose for each one of us, as you bring us into your glorious light and understanding of who we are meant to be. Live in us and allow us to reflect your light and majesty to those who surround us. Allow us to lead many back to you as you draw them and we will comfort them as they turn their hearts towards you God, our Father. Amen.

My love is being poured out now around the world as many experience it for the first time. It is with much excitement that I look forward to having many hearts turned to me to lead them in a way never before known.

They will begin to feel a new sense of complete and utter joy as my Spirit and love lives within their heart and they begin to see the purpose for mankind here on earth.

Many will be changed from the inside out and will become a new creation as they continue to look to me for strength and the forgiveness of sins.

My child I know how much you long to have all mankind in this place of peace and worship and I too look forward in eager anticipation as the day fast approaches.

Do not give up hope and do not neglect your calling. Know that the time fast approaches and will be upon us very soon. I will require your total heartfelt commitment in order to achieve my Father's will. It is through your complete obedience to my Holy Spirit that I am able to carry out God's will in your life.

Be still my child and trust in me. Do not fret or worry for I shall tell you when the time is right and you will know. Be at peace and rest in God as you continue to carry out the work that he has destined for you to do.

Shabbat Shalom

SALVATION PRAYER

Dear Lord Jesus

Suddenly I am aware of who you are. I have eyes to see and ears to hear all that you have to show me personally. I was lost but now I'm found.

Please show me the way. Please help me to restore my relationship with God the Father. Please forgive me of my sins and please Lord Jesus be that beautiful lamb of God that was sacrificed in order for my sins to be forgiven.

I now ask you into my life and surrender my heart. I now ask you to come and live your life within me. Teach me, show me the way in which you want me to go while here on earth. Your will be done in my life here on earth.

Shabbat Shalom

www.ingramcontent.com/pod-product-compliance
Lightning Source LLC
Chambersburg PA
CBHW060526100426
42743CB00009B/1437